THE SECRET PLACE

BEVERLY UEBERT ANGEL

LEVI HOUSE

ISBN 978-1-7399735-1-3

CONTENTS

ONE
HIDDEN IN PLAIN SIGHT

"My Secret Place is not some hidden, concealed or mysterious thing as many of My children have been led to believe. My people have been fed a lie. The Secret Place is not even a place of consecration where one gets to have deep intimacy with Me. It simply is not." God spoke as clear as day.

The time was 05:32 am in a city of contrasts, an eclectic mix of shiny hotels and swanky office blocks neighbouring beautiful, red-tiled colonial-era buildings. We were in the nation's capital, Colombo, a city determined to reclaim its 19th-century moniker, 'the garden city of the East.' Like old Eden, it seemed to be the best place for God to speak to me about the Secret Place. We had just started our two-day Good News Sri Lanka Conference, and thousands upon thousands had converged upon the city of Colombo for this landmark gathering of Christians.

"It takes maturity to know that the Secret Place is not something you pray yourself into. You have heard in My word that when the heir is still a child, he differs nothing from a servant. So the problem with the Secret Place is simply immaturity in My people."

That statement from the mouth of the Master that early morning hit home. I remembered that when I was a little girl, I used to believe that if I could not see you, you could not see me. So, I would hide—or what I thought was hiding —in plain view. I would get behind something, not realizing that my feet or some other obvious body part were still visible. But as long as my eyes were hidden, I believed that since I could not see the person I was hiding from, they could not see me either. Imagine how surprised I was every time they would walk right up to me and find me in my "hiding place."

My childish predicament was not unique to me. It is a humorous albeit understandable phenomenon that we see in young children. As long as their eyes are hidden, they believe that they become magically invisible. Their perspective is dictated by their limited understanding of their surroundings. So, instead of becoming masters of hiding in their secret place, they fail to recognize that their secret place is only secret to those who cannot see that they're in it. This is a level of discernment and consciousness that many Christians do not have. That is precisely why the understanding of God's Secret Place has eluded them.

Psalm 91 is arguably one of the most read or recited passages of scripture in the Bible. People use it like spiritual self-defence spray in hopes of keeping demonic villainous activity at bay. For many, it is analogous to a biblical rabbit's foot used to ward off bad luck by those who deem themselves to be vulnerable to such. The very fact that anyone would try to "use" the secret place in any way is proof that they do not yet understand what it is. That is why we have Christians fasting and praying to get into the secret place. They believe that they will find God in His Secret Place, yet they have failed to find Him even though He has left body parts still showing. That means that Christians are either not aware the Secret Place exists, or they're searching for it in the wrong places, or they are looking right at it but do not recognize it.

The Bible is replete with esoteric information, fenced-in privileged information, that is reserved for exclusive access. The revelation contained in it is, in fact, gifted to an esoteric people, and it is our privilege and responsibility as Christians to unwrap that gift. This is what the scripture is talking about in Proverbs 25, verse 2, where it says:

Proverbs 25:2

It is the glory of God to conceal a thing: but the honour of kings is to search out a matter.

That verse speaks volumes about the ways of God. They are not mysterious, as many suppose. He reveals His ways to us throughout the scriptures and tells us clearly how He operates. This verse is one of many examples of that. It says it is the glory of God to conceal a thing. Think about that. God conceals or hides things, and the Bible calls it His glory when He does that. Why do you suppose He would tell us that He conceals things? The next part of the verse tells us: He wants us to "search out a matter."

The words "thing" and "matter" are both translated from the Hebrew word *dabar*, which refers to His Word. So, what is God saying? Obviously, He has not hidden His Word from you. You have sixty-six books of the Bible that contain the Word of God. But within the Word that He has given to us, there is revelation that is only accessible by searching out a matter.

You see, God is not a tease. He does not tell you He's hidden things just to taunt you with that information. He is telling you that there is revelation He has hidden in His Word that is reserved for those who will search for it, not that it's hidden, but it's hidden in plain sight. Such is the case with the Secret Place.

So, what is the Secret Place, and how do we dwell there? That is what I, through the Holy Ghost, and as the Lord poured into me that morning in Colombo, will show you in this book. Let's begin by taking a closer look at the scripture in Psalm 91, verse 1. There is something I want to show you there.

Psalm 91:1

He that dwelleth in the secret place of the most High shall abide under the shadow of the Almighty.

First of all, let me start by making it clear that the Secret Place is not a geographical location. It is not a physical place where you can say I am going from here to there. Neither is it a religious place where you go to seek God, nor a hidden place where you escape the noise of society and the troubles of this life. It is actually a place where the mystery of oneness is achieved so that God and man can become one, existing as co-heirs of the purposes of God. However, that cannot be achieved except and unless we understand that the Secret Place is not a location.

The words translated "secret place" in Psalm 91 are derived from the Hebrew word *cathar* or *satar*. To get a fuller understanding of what that word means, we need to examine it a bit more closely.

Satar in Hebrew is spelt ***samech tav resh*** (read from right to left). Now, in order to understand the significance of each of these letters, you must first understand that Hebrew, as with other ancient languages, uses pictographic script. That means there are pictures that symbolize what each letter means. I'm going to break these down, and I want you to stay with me on this as it's so important for you to catch this part in order to fully grasp the Secret Place revelation. Samech looks like a little rounded vessel with a flat roof or cover.

Samech

The ancient sages picture this as a shelter. It literally means to surround or support, like a hug. The rounded vessel represents the heart of God, and when you get into His heart, He places a cover over it, and you are protected. Just by looking at the meaning of samech, we can already start to see the Secret Place in a new light. When the psalmist speaks of those who dwell in the *satar* of God, he is referring to those who find shelter in the very heart of God. When you are in the Secret Place, you are in a place of supreme protection right in the heart of God, surrounded and supported by Him. What a beautiful picture that is!

Right next to *samech* is the letter *tav*. This is the last letter of the Hebrew alphabet, and it is described as the shape of a seal or a stamp.

Tav

Tav represents the truth or knowledge of God. It speaks of the Word of God that is revealed. According to Hebrew sages, God's stamp or seal is truth. In the ancient pictographic script, this letter is a picture of two sticks in the shape of a cross that is used as a sign or a marker.

Ezekiel saw a vision where those who were found righteous in Israel were given a mark on their forehead, and they were spared when destruction came.

Ezekiel 9:4, 6a

And the Lord said unto him, Go through the midst of the city, through the midst of Jerusalem, and set a mark upon the foreheads of the men that sigh and that cry for all the abominations that be done in the midst thereof.

Slay utterly old and young, both maids, and little children, and women: but come not near any man upon whom is the mark.

The word translated "mark" in those two verses is tav. And if you read through all of Ezekiel chapter 9, you will see that everyone did not receive tav. Likewise, in the Secret Place, we find support and protection in the heart of God, but it is only found by those who receive the revelation of the truth of God.

Now, there is one more letter we need to look at in the word samech, and that's the letter *resh*. The symbol behind the shape of the letter resh is a bowed head, someone bent over in service.

Resh

That is symbolic of the Holy Spirit. Jesus, in John chapter 14, verse 26, calls the Holy Spirit the Helper.

John 14:26

But the Comforter, which is the Holy Ghost, whom the Father will send in my name, he shall teach you all things, and bring all things to your remembrance, whatsoever I have said unto you.

Now, if you read that verse only in the King James Version, you will not see the word 'helper' there, but it is hidden in the word 'Comforter.' Let me show that verse to you in the classic Amplified version so you can see it clearly.

John 14:26

But the Comforter (Counselor, *Helper* [emphasis added], Intercessor, Advocate, Strengthener, Standby), the Holy Spirit, Whom the Father will send in My name [in My place, to represent Me and act on My behalf], He will teach you all things. And He will cause you to recall (will remind you of, bring to your remembrance) everything I have told you.

Do you see it now? The Holy Spirit is the Helper. The Bible tells us that Jesus came in the form of a servant. He did not come to be served, but to serve. We find that in Mark chapter 10, verse 45:

Mark 10:45

For even the Son of man came not to be ministered unto, but to minister, and to give his life a ransom for many.

It says He came to "minister." That's the Greek word *diakonéō*, which means to be *an attendant* or *serve*. Then Jesus turns around and tells us that He will give us another Comforter, the Holy Spirit, someone who is just like Him, *állos paráklētos*. That means the Holy Spirit also came to serve just as Jesus did.

The term "the secret place" in Hebrew means exactly that: a hidden or secret place. It would not be a secret place if it were out in the open or evident. So, this secret place must be a place that is not readily seen by everyone. However, God has left parts showing so that we can find it. He has left us *samech*, *tav*, and *resh* to show us that the Secret Place is not a 'what' but a 'who.' The Secret Place is none other than the **Lord Jesus Christ**!

The revelation of the Secret Place as a person is the accurate revelation of scripture. And the highest purpose of the Secret Place is to attain the mystery of oneness. The mystery of oneness is what defines the reality of the Godhead. The reality and government of the Triune God are regulated by the mystery of oneness, how the three can be one. So, what God wants to achieve by the reality and the operation of the Secret Place is to bring us to a place of oneness. That is not possible without understanding and recognizing the Secret Place as the person of Jesus Christ.

Jesus is the One who embraces us and brings us into the heart of God. Look at what He says of Himself in John chapter 16, verse 28:

John 16:28a

I came forth from the Father, and am come into the world:

Not only did Jesus come forth from the Father, but He is also the very expression—the embodiment—of the Father's heart. He came to reveal the Father's heart to us.

It is only when you catch the revelation of who Jesus is that your eyes are opened to the Secret Place. That is why *tav* is so important. The revelation of who Jesus is comes from the knowledge of the Word of God. In John 14, verse 6, Jesus says:

John 14:6a

I am the way, the *truth* [emphasis added], and the life.

Jesus *is* the Truth! This is not truth that you can know by mere deductive reasoning or intellectual comprehension. Look at what the Bible says in Colossians 2, verse 3:

Colossians 2:3

In whom are hid all the treasures of wisdom and knowledge.

Do you see that? *All* the treasures of wisdom and knowledge are hid in Christ. And that word 'hid' means *kept secret*. In other words, He is the Secret Place in whom all the treasures of wisdom and knowledge are kept. Not some of the treasures, all of them. There is no truth to talk about unless you have a revelation of who Jesus is. And this is where **resh** comes in.

The Bible says that the Holy Spirit is the One who leads us into all truth. Not some truth, not part of the truth, but the *whole* truth, and that Truth is a Person. You cannot receive a revelation of who Jesus is without the Holy Spirit leading and guiding you into Truth. The Holy Spirit is the Spirit of Truth who shines the spotlight on who Jesus is. He glorifies Him. That's what Jesus says in John chapter 16, verses 13 and 15:

John 16:13, 15a

Howbeit when He, the Spirit of truth, is come, He will guide you into all truth... He shall glorify Me.

The Holy Spirit has come to give you a revelation of who Jesus is. One aspect of that revelation is that Jesus is the Secret Place.

Let me remind you that Hebrew is read from right to left. So when we look at the spelling of the word *satar*, we understand that the letters *samech tav resh* are read from right to left (samech being the rightmost letter).

But when we look at the pictographic representation of the letters, we also see a progression that starts with resh, then leads to tav, and ends with samech.

Without *resh*, the Spirit of Truth, you cannot get to *tav*, the revelation of truth which comes from the knowledge of the Word of God. That revelation leads you to *samech* who is Jesus, the heart of God.

Now, let's go back to Psalm 91, and with that understanding of *satar* (the Secret Place), let's look at verses 1 and 2.

Psalm 91:1-2

He that dwelleth in the secret place of the most High shall abide under the shadow of the Almighty. I will say of the Lord, He is my refuge and my fortress: my God; in him will I trust.

Notice it says that the one who dwells in the Secret Place shall abide under the shadow of the Almighty. That is not referring to two different things, but one. The Secret Place and the Shadow of the Almighty are synonymous. Just as you cannot separate a shadow from the person from whom it is cast, you cannot separate the Shadow of the Almighty from the Secret Place.

The Shadow of the Almighty represents the oneness that we have in Christ. Paul says it this way:

1 Corinthians 6:17

But he that is joined unto the Lord is one spirit.

That verse gives us the key to dwelling in the Secret Place. The Secret Place is not something you have to search for. If you are in Christ, you are already in it. You are one with Him, hidden in the Secret Place. Simply put, you are already in the Secret Place. That is why the Bible says that we are hidden with Him. Notice what Colossians 3, verse 3 says:

Colossians 3:3

For ye are dead, and your life is hid with Christ in God.

Your life is also hidden because it is in Christ who is the Secret (or hidden) Place. If you are in the Secret Place, you are also under the Shadow of the Almighty. Knowing the Secret Place is a wonderful revelation, but revelation without application is merely information. Therefore, we need to understand the spiritual implications and relevance of being in the Secret Place.

What I have shown you so far is the address of the Secret Place. It is Jesus. But Psalm 91, verse 1 does not say, He who knows the address of the Secret Place shall abide under the Shadow of the Almighty. It says, He who *dwells* in the Secret Place. There is a difference between knowing an address and living there. There are also benefits to dwelling at an address. So, the question we need to explore is how do you dwell in the Secret Place? Let's continue to search out the matter so that we can benefit from all the privileges of dwelling in the Secret Place.

TWO
RIGHT OF ABODE

Deportation did not start with Immigration Offices. It started with God. Enoch was the first person to be deported for violating his permanent residency status. He was an upstanding citizen of Earth, exemplary in character, even a prophet of God. But he had one problem: he enjoyed spending too much time outside of his country, Earth. The Bible puts it this way, "Enoch walked with God" (Genesis 5:24).

You see, Enoch had Indefinite Leave to Remain on Earth. But the problem with Indefinite Leave to Remain is that it restricts how long you can be away from your country of residency. Enoch spent so much time with God that his residency on earth was revoked. That is why He could not return. The Bible says, "**he was not; for God took him**" (Genesis 5:24). While many are seeking Indefinite Leave to Remain, or a green card or permanent residence where they are, some, like Enoch, have realized that there is a far superior residence status.

Let me give our church as an example. Spirit Embassy is a coat of many colours. We call it that because we have congregants from all over the world, different races, different cultures, and so on. Some of whom seek to establish permanent residency in the United Kingdom where some of our branches are located. So, we've had over the years many requests for my husband Prophet Angel and I to pray that they might be granted Indefinite Leave to Remain (permanent stay or residence). We do not pray, however, because we are a solution ground for visas. Just by entering the doors, we know that all immigration problems are sorted by faith. The plethora of testimonies that follow confirm that our God certainly works at the Home Office (U.K. immigration or any other for that matter). Those who desire Indefinite Leave to Remain receive it, often with supernatural speed and delivery.

Indefinite Leave to Remain, otherwise known as settlement or settling, gives you the right to live and work in the UK as long as you want. This, for many people born outside of Britain, is the ultimate immigration status. But there are restrictions that can cause you to lose your permanent residency status. For example, at the time of writing this book, if you leave the country for more than two years, eyebrows are raised as to why you deserve to return when you clearly prefer being elsewhere. Or, if you commit an offence, it's almost guaranteed that your permanent residency will be revoked. So, as it turns out, permanent residence, as established by the UK's definition of Indefinite Leave to Remain, is not so permanent after all. No wonder the government calls it settling.

However, those with the Right of Abode do not have such restrictions. They are free to go and come as they please.

And they can live abroad for as long as they want, even commit a crime and be punished for it, but still not have their Right of Abode revoked. This is because all British citizens automatically have Right of Abode in the UK. They do not have to apply for it; they are born into it.

There is something notable about having a permanent abode. In Psalm 91, verse 1, the psalmist says:

Psalm 91:1

He that dwelleth in the Secret Place of the most High shall abide under the shadow of the Almighty.

That verse tells us that everyone does not have the privilege of abiding under the shadow of the Almighty. Notice the verse says only those who dwell in the Secret Place have the right to abide under the shadow of the Almighty. It is a benefit of dwelling in the Secret Place.

The Secret Place is not a spiritual level or dimension that you go in and out of. Always keep this in mind: the Secret Place is none other than the Lord Jesus Christ. Dwelling there is a spiritual positioning. That is why comments such as "I'm going into the Spirit," or "I'm seeking the Presence" are indicative of a lack of understanding. You do not have to *get* there. If you are a Christian, you were *born* there.

The Bible tells us that we are born of the Spirit. Look at what Jesus says in John chapter 3, verses 5 and 6:

John 3:5-6

Jesus answered, Verily, verily, I say unto thee, Except a man be born of water and of the Spirit, he cannot enter into the kingdom of God. That which is born of the flesh is flesh; and that which is born of the Spirit is spirit.

You are born of the Spirit. Yes, you are housed in a body, but you are a spiritual being, and you dwell in a spiritual location called Christ.

Paul picks this up in Romans chapter 8, where he says:

Romans 8:8-9

So then they that are in the flesh cannot please God. But *ye are not in the flesh, but in the Spirit* [emphasis added], if so be that the Spirit of God dwell in you. Now if any man have not the Spirit of Christ, he is none of his.

You are in the Spirit – not when you pray, not when you fast, not when you go to the mountain for seven days, but always. Just as the Right of Abode is automatically given to those who are born into the UK, the right to abide under the shadow of the Almighty is automatically granted to those who are born into Jesus Christ, the Secret Place.

Right now, you have Indefinite Leave to Remain in your physical body. It is a "permanent" residence, but with restrictions. Your residency can be revoked. If you agree with sickness, that can become your immigration officer who deems you a visitor and revokes your residency. If you commit a crime against your physical body, depending on the severity of the offence, your residency can be revoked. And we know that if your spirit leaves your body for too long, you will definitely be deported to another location. But there is nothing and no one that can revoke your right of abode in Christ.

To better understand this, let's look more closely at the words *dwell* and *abide* from Psalm 91, verse 1. Looking at the two words in the English language, it might appear that they are the same. However, they are not. The word translated "dwelleth" is from the Hebrew word *yashab*, which means to *sit down*.

Now, it is important to note that in the biblical Hebrew language, there is no past, present, or future tense. Those are all related to time. There is only what is called perfect and imperfect tense, which are both related to action. The perfect tense refers to a completed action, and an imperfect tense is an action that is not completed. For example, the word "dwelleth" in Psalm 91:1 is in the perfect tense. So, what does all of that mean? It means that the dwelling part is already done. You have sat down in Christ. You are not trying to dwell there. It is where you already are.

The Bible tells us in Ephesians 2, verse 6, that we are seated with Christ in heavenly places.

Ephesians 2:6

And hath raised us up together, and made us sit together in heavenly places in Christ Jesus.

Notice it says He "*hath... made* us sit." It's already done. So, what about the "abide" part of Psalm 91:1? That is translated from the Hebrew word *luwn*, which means *to stay overnight*. That first definition does not mean that the Secret Place is like a hotel you check in and out of. Abiding in the Secret Place indicates permanency. In fact, another literal meaning is *to stay permanently*.

Christ is your permanent abode. With that understanding in mind, Psalm 91:1 could be accurately read this way:

Psalm 91:1

He that *sat down* in Christ shall *stay permanently* under the shadow of the Almighty.

Do you see it now? Dwelling in the Secret Place, who is Jesus, is having an awareness of the reality that you are in Him. It is a *sunesis* (or mindset) that is governed by the knowledge that He is your permanent abode. You are in Christ. Therefore, when you declare Psalm 91, verse 1, that is not a confession. You are not saying it to try to make it so. Rather, it is an affirmation of a reality that this verse is talking about you, the born-again Christian who is seated permanently in Christ.

In the Church, many Christians are seeking Indefinite Leave to Remain in the Secret Place, not realizing they have already been granted the Right of Abode. This lack of awareness is why you hear of so many saying things like "we are seeking the presence of God," or we are "going into the Spirit." You are not entering the presence of God or getting in the Spirit. You were born there. You abide there. The Secret Place is your permanent, eternal residence.

THREE
THE SECRET OF THE SHADOW

When I started working on this book again after shelving it for some time, we were at the start of the COVID-19 global pandemic. Efforts to control the spread of the coronavirus caused officials to enact measures that supposedly limited our exposure to the virus. The world was on lockdown, and most of its global citizens were sheltered in their homes, homes previously considered to be places of protection. Unfortunately for some, they brought the virus in with them. So, even though they were in their homes, what should be a place of protection became an incubator for sickness, disease, and death. Their houses were not able to "protect" them after all.

You see, your place of protection is only as secure as that which can guarantee the preservation of your wellbeing. For example, a physical house is only as secure as its inhabitants. That is why you can have a house that is armed with the most cutting-edge security technology, and someone can still break in if the occupants of the home forget to activate the alarm system.

Many Christians read Psalm 91 and think that the "shadow" of the Almighty is some sort of supernatural security system, and that is where they miss it. The shadow itself is as inconsequential as a house with a security system that is inactivated. It has no power of its own. The focus should not be on the shadow of the Almighty for one simple reason: He has no shadow as most understand a shadow to be.

In order for a shadow to be visible, three things must be present: an opaque object, a light source, and darkness. A shadow can only be cast when you have an object that blocks the light. Not every object can do that. Some objects allow light to pass through, and such objects cannot cast shadows. Only an opaque object can cast a shadow.

God, by His very nature, defies the laws of physics and optics. The Bible clearly tells us in John chapter 4, verse 24, that "**God is a Spirit**." He does not have a physical or opaque body; therefore, it is physically impossible for Him to have a shadow.

Not only does there need to be an opaque object to cast a shadow, but a light source and darkness is also required for a shadow to be visible. The Bible tells us that God is light. We see that in 1 John chapter 1, in the first part of verse 5, which says:

1 John 1:5a

This then is the message which we have heard of him, and declare unto you, that God is light...

He is the source of all light. But the verse does not stop there. Let's read through to the end:

1 John 1:5

This then is the message which we have heard of him, and declare unto you, that God is light, *and in him is no darkness at all* [emphasis added].

Remember, to cast a shadow, you need an opaque object, a light source, and darkness. If you have one without the other two, it is impossible to cast a shadow. God, who is a Spirit, is not opaque. And although He is Light and the source of all light, He cannot cast a shadow because there is no darkness in Him at all. James affirms this in chapter 1, verse 17 of his epistle, where he says:

James 1:17

Every good gift and every perfect gift is from above, and cometh down from the Father of lights, with whom is no variableness, neither shadow of turning.

God is the Father or source or originator of lights. Furthermore, the Bible says that with Him, there is no *variableness* or *shadow of turning*.

When the scripture speaks of 'variableness,' it is the Greek word *parallagé*, which means *transmutation*, a very scientific word. It means a change from one state of being to another usually degraded state of being. So, when the Bible says there is no variableness with God, it is telling you that

God remains in an unalterable state of being that can never be degraded. He is Light that cannot be transmuted into darkness.

Then it says that with God, there is no *shadow of turning*. The word 'shadow' is rendered from the Greek word *aposkíasma*, a compound of the words *apo*, which means *off* and *skia*, which means *shade* or *darkness*. So, it literally means *a shading off*. James is telling us that there is nothing in God that can cause such obscuration or shading off of light. God, who is Light, cannot be blocked.

A shadow is an interruption of light, which is an inconceivable notion when it comes to God. He is the God who calls light out of darkness, not darkness out of light. The Bible says the Light shines in darkness, and the darkness comprehends—*katalambánō*—it not (John 1:5). Darkness cannot get a hold of God and do anything with Him. Therefore, no shadow can be cast from Him. Why then would the scripture talk about the "shadow" of the Almighty?

I said earlier that a place of protection is only as powerful as that which can guarantee your preservation. That is why it is so important to understand who "the Almighty" is, because it is in the Almighty, and not the shadow, that protection is found. Yes, we know the Almighty is God, but in His sovereignty, He allowed the writer of the psalm to use that specific title in reference to Him. So, the question we should be asking is "Why?"

The "Almighty" is the Hebrew word *Shadday* or *Shaddai* which means, the *Many Breasted One*. Why would God choose this particular title in this context? What does the

Many Breasted One have to do with protection? This is the secret and significance of the shadow.

When you have a natural shadow, the closer you are to the light source, the larger the shadow it casts. This is because an object closer to the source will block a larger area of the light. But I have already made it clear that God does not cast any shadows, neither can His light be blocked. The shadow represents protection that is the result of an intimate connection. You are in Christ, as close as you can ever be to the Light source, who is El Shaddai; and therefore, you are supremely protected.

El Shaddai, the Many Breasted One, paints a picture of God as a nursing mother. It is not coincidental that He chose this specific imagery to convey the idea of protection. A mother's milk is loaded with benefits that protect the child. It strengthens the child's immunity; it helps them avoid diseases and protects them from harmful agents. It is the purest and most potent defence system imaginable. And it is made possible by the intimate connection between the nursing mother—the breasted one—and the child.

When a mother is nursing her child, she first draws the child as close to herself as she possibly can. But before the child can get the benefits of the mother's milk, a process called latching takes place.

Latching is a process where the baby's head must be positioned towards the mother so that it can draw milk from the mother's breast. That is the first phase of the latching process. Sometimes the baby is fussing and crying, not realising that the very thing it's crying for is right there. So, it is necessary for the child to turn to, and have an awareness of, the "breasted one," the one who provides protection.

As Christians, we do not need to fuss and cry for protection. We need only realise that we are already in the place where ultimate protection is found. We are in the Secret Place, in Christ, where God the Father has drawn us close to His bosom. There is no greater or more intimate positioning than that. It requires only an awakening to that reality for us to then shift our focus to the One who has everything we need to sustain and protect us.

Once the child is aware of and focused on the "breasted one," the next phase of the latching process happens: the baby must open its mouth. No matter how much protection is available in the mother's milk, it will not benefit the child unless it gets inside. And that won't happen unless the child opens its mouth. The psalmist says it this way:

Psalm 91:2

I will say **[emphasis added] of the Lord, He is my refuge and my fortress: my God; in him will I trust.**

To latch on to the Breasted One, your mouth must be open, declaring who He is. And this is not a mere parting of the lips; you have to open your mouth wide. Psalm 81, verse 10 says, "**open your mouth wide, and I will fill it.**" So when protection is needed, we do not look at the problem and tell God how great the problem is. Instead, we look at the problem and declare to it how great our God is!

When we open our mouths and bless the Lord, we draw from His benefits. The Bible says it this way in Psalm 103, verses 1 through 5:

Psalm 103:1-5

Bless the Lord, O my soul: and all that is within me, bless his holy name. Bless the Lord, O my soul, and forget not all his benefits: Who forgiveth all thine iniquities; who healeth all thy diseases; Who redeemeth thy life from destruction; who crowneth thee with lovingkindness and tender mercies; *Who satisfieth thy mouth with good things* **[emphasis added]; so that thy youth is renewed like the eagle's.**

It is a spiritual principle: you have what you say. You receive what God has for you by faith and with an open mouth. His forgiveness, healing, preservation, safety and protection are all inside Him. However, it is with your mouth that you appropriate those benefits. Just as the immunity of the mother is passed to the child as he draws from what's inside her, in a similar way, the divine antibodies of God flow into you as you open your mouth and declare who He is and His benefits.

Using this Hebrew concept of the shadow, God is assuring you of absolute protection that can only be found in Him. And as we continue further into our examination of Psalm 91, you will see that He breaks down the different facets of protection as well as the timings. Ultimately, He promises you protection against disease, any form of terror, and all the powers of darkness. Once you have the revelation that you are already in the Secret Place of the Most High, you could be in the most dangerous place in the world, and it will not matter. No place escapes His protection.

Reverting to our earlier analogy, a nursing child is oblivious to anything other than its intimate connection to its mother. They are only aware of their closeness to the one who supplies what is needed for their protection, comfort, and preservation. You also must increase your awareness of your intimate connection to the Breasted One. Only then will you abide under the shadow of the Almighty and live in the consciousness of His complete protection.

The Word of God has painted for us a picture of supreme supernatural immunity and absolute protection, which are the result of God's love for you. Knowing that God loves you enough to protect you from all harm casts out every fear. But these benefits will not be realised fully until you are aware of your connection with Him. Then you will open your mouth and take what is inside the Breasted One inside you. Life, peace, comfort, protection, and preservation all reside in El Shaddai. And it is through your intimate connection with Him that you are sheltered and abide under His shadow.

Now, we have seen that the secret of the shadow of the Almighty is not only protection, but also the intimacy with Him which makes that protection possible. However, there is yet another level of intimacy greater than what has already been depicted. This is the intimacy that most desire, but few are privileged to acquire.

FOUR

A FORETASTE OF GLORY

Your gender can make you want to miss the rapture. As glorious as the thought of Heaven is, some Christians are not ready to go there. It is not that they are unsaved or that they do not love Jesus. They are indeed born again. But they are not ready for the rapture to happen now for one simple reason: they are gender identified. Their maleness or femaleness clouds their ability to comprehend that there could be anything greater than a man and a woman coming together in sexual intimacy.

If you were to interview a group of unmarried Christians and ask them why they desire to be married, you would get the stock answers. Some will say that they desire to be with someone because they want "companionship," or they want to "settle down" and have a family. There is nothing wrong with desiring such things. But the truth of the matter is, most men and women want to get married because they want to enjoy the freedom of sexual intimacy without guilt or fear of sinning. If sexual intimacy were removed from the equation, the desire to get married would likely suffer a sharp decline.

Scarcity can directly increase the perception of value. Limited editions, for example, bring a higher price tag than those things which are commonly found. Good relationships these days seem to have become limited editions. From the world's perspective, the odds are against you if you are still single and desire a monogamous relationship with a person of the opposite sex. Even the prophet Isaiah foretold that seven women will lay claim to one man. You will find that in Isaiah 54:1, which says:

Isaiah 54:1

And in that day seven women shall take hold of one man, saying, We will eat our own bread, and wear our own apparel: only let us be called by thy name, to take away our reproach.

Seven to one is not the best odds. Statistics like those often leave men and women alike feeling disheartened, even pushing some to the brink of desperation. According to world population data, the ratio of men to women is neck and neck currently. That is to say, there are nearly as many men as there are women. However, the increase of blurred lines between males and females, along with the rise of same-sex relationships, make the odds seem otherwise.

The desire for intimacy is potent. So powerful, in fact, that even though the great move of the rapture is imminent, some, like Lot's wife, are already looking at what they will leave behind. They cannot imagine that the God who created sexual intimacy could ever come up with a better idea. They fail to remember that this is the God who makes no two snowflakes alike, no two people alike, no two fingerprints alike. Of all the billions of human beings that ever existed on Earth, no two are the same, not even identical twins. Imagine that!

God is the master of prolific ideation. There is no shortage of good ideas with Him. He is the Genesis of every genesis, the Creator of creativity, the Inventor of imagination. He is such a wonder that the angels never cease to cry, "Holy! Holy! Holy!" Every time they behold Him, they see another facet of His wondrous being that they have never seen before since time immemorial. In a place where there is no time, they experience unending fascination and immense, overwhelming joy because of the incredible manifestations of the unique mind of this glorious God!

Without the awareness of the magnificent creative ability of God, whose love for you is unmatched, you might be tempted to believe that you are giving up something of great value that can never be replaced or surpassed. God in His goodness allows us to enjoy unique experiences with Him while we are in this earthly body. The apostle Paul puts it like this in Romans chapter 8, verse 23:

Romans 8:23 AMPC

And not only the creation, but we ourselves too, who have and enjoy the firstfruits of the [Holy] Spirit [a foretaste of the blissful things to come] groan inwardly as we wait for the redemption of our bodies [from sensuality and the grave, which will reveal]

our adoption (our manifestation as God's sons).

There are experiences that we can have right here on Earth that serve as previews of coming attractions, each a "foretaste of the blissful things to come."

We understand that what we enjoy here on Earth is only a shadow of the joys that await us. There is, however, an intimacy that you can experience right now that is incomparable to anything you will ever experience in Heaven. Why? Because it is reserved exclusively for you while you are on Earth. You can enjoy an ongoing honeymoon experience, guilt-free, whether you are married or single. In short, what I am saying is, God wants to be intimate with you.

Now, I want you to raise your thinking to another level. Remember, God is a Spirit. I am simply using language you can understand to communicate and convey the intensity of a profound revelation. You see, God craves intimacy with you more than a soon-to-be newlywed couple anticipates the consummation of their marriage on their wedding day.

When you are getting married, you prepare for your wedding and the celebration that follows the marriage ceremony. But the thing you anticipate the most is the honeymoon. After all the festivities have ended, and all of the guests have gone, the moment you have been waiting for arrives. You enter your bedroom knowing that there is nothing keeping you from being with each other. It is a sacred place and time set aside for you to come together. You can bare all, free to fully know and experience one another. In those moments, you will whisper words that are for your beloved's ears only. It is a level of intimacy that you share with no one else in this private place that is reserved for your time together. Such is the intimacy of the Secret Place.

You are already in this Place but you may not recognize where you were. I will show its location from the scripture in Matthew chapter 6, verse 6, which says:

Matthew 6:6

But thou, when thou prayest, enter into thy closet, and when thou hast shut thy door, pray to thy Father which is in secret; and thy Father which seeth in secret shall reward thee openly.

Jesus' reference here to your "closet" is a vital key to understanding the intimacy of the Secret Place. When Jesus said that you are to "enter into thy closet," many have missed the significance of what He meant. Was He telling you to get up every morning, open your closet door, shove all your clothes and shoes to the side, crawl inside, shut the door, and pray? Of course not! To capture the profundity of what He was communicating, we must look at the etymology of the word 'closet' more closely.

The word 'closet' is rendered from the Greek word *tameion*, an old word that has an interesting progression in history. At first, the word tameion was used to depict a secret place where one would hide his or her most valuable possessions. But as time progressed, it became a word to describe a secure place where a person could put money or treasure, such as a safety deposit box or a vault at the bank. Finally, by New Testament times, tameion came to describe a private inner chamber or bedroom.

Intimate moments are shared in the bedroom. It is a secret place where a treasured relationship takes place between a husband and his wife. When a husband and wife enter their bedroom to be with each other, no one else is allowed. It is a private place and experience to be shared only between husband and wife. The word tameion is used in this sense to convey the idea of intimacy with God in prayer. With that imagery in mind, Matthew 6, verse 6 could be translated:

> **When it is time for you to pray, enter into your bedroom, and when you have shut the door behind you and secured a place of privacy, then pray ... .**

Just as a husband and wife enter their bedroom and shut the door so they can bare their hearts and souls to each other, you also ought to have a relationship with the Lord that is so tender, so special, and so intimate, that it is shared only between you and Him and no one else.

The Secret Place is all about intimacy, fellowship, and oneness with Christ. And prayer is a practice – an expression – of that intimacy. It would be inconceivable to understand that the Secret Place is the Person of Jesus Christ and not spend time with Him in prayer. The person who understands the revelation of the Secret Place is a person of prayer. You do not pray to enter the Secret Place. You pray because you are in the Secret Place. Prayer is the consummation of your oneness with Christ. In prayer, you give yourself to Him, and He gives Himself to you.

When you enter into a serious time of prayer, it should be done at a place and time when you are not interrupted so the Holy Spirit can speak to your heart, and you can bare your heart to Him. It is a time of personal rapture, a mingling together of your spirit with the Holy Spirit. It does not matter where you spend this private time with the Lord; it just matters that you do it.

Susanna Wesley, the mother of the great and notable evangelists John and Charles Wesley, had a total of nineteen children. You can only imagine how busy her daily life must have been. But she knew how to steal away and spend time in the Secret Place. Remember, we are not talking here about her *entering into* a secret place but enjoying the Secret Place, which is Christ, because that is where she already was.

As her children read, studied, or played, her Darling Lover would call for her to come and be with Him. Unable to physically leave her little ones, she would sit down in a chair, throw her kitchen apron over her head, and commune with the lover of her soul in her own special private prayer "closet." She understood the Secret Place was not a physical location but the Person of Christ. The children recognizing that their mother was no longer in the kitchen but fellowshipping with Christ, the Secret Place, knew not to disturb or distract her.

Jesus often arose early in the morning to pray when the disciples were still sleeping. He would pray on a mountaintop or out in the wilderness, far from the hustle and bustle of the city. There is nothing in the Bible that says the early morning hours are more holy than other hours of the day. And nowhere does the Bible teach that praying on a mountaintop is somehow better than other places. Jesus chose those early morning hours because it was when He could find solitude and quietness with God. He prayed on the mountaintops and in the wilderness because those isolated places allowed Him to pray without interference. No Wi-Fi, no phone, no radio – nothing. Just intimacy with the Father.

Jesus portrays prayer as something so precious that it should occur in a bedroom with the door shut. This does not literally mean you must pray in a bedroom any more than it means you must pray in a closet. The point is that the "closet" is free from interruption, distraction, and listening ears. The concept of a bedroom is used to convey the idea of an isolated and solitary place where you spend intimate alone time with the Lord. The key is intimacy with Him.

Your prayer "closet" may be in your car when you drive to work every morning because that's the only time and place you can find to be alone. It may be in the shower as you prepare for the day. It may be early in the morning when everyone else in the house is still sleeping. Or you may find it better to pray late at night after others have gone to bed and you are finally alone. Have a quiet place and a sacred time when you can give yourself wholly to God in prayer and allow Him to have fellowship with you.

You may say, "I know I need to spend quality time with the Lord, but my schedule is so busy that it's hard for me to find a time to do it." But the truth is, you find time for other things that you deem important. Think about it. Do you read the newspaper or watch the news? Do you watch television programs or find time to stream movies? Do you make time in your schedule for recreation or exercise? You make time for whatever is important to you. So, if you really want to have an intimate, personal relationship with the Lord, you will find time for that as well.

Intimacy with Him must be consciously and intentionally cultivated. Make it a daily priority to have times of communion with the Father through the Holy Spirit. It is there that you will discover why the psalmist in Psalm 16, verse 11 declared:

Psalm 16:11

In Your presence there is fulness of joy, and at Your right hand are pleasures for evermore.

Find a time of the day when you can put everything else aside and concentrate only on Him. Select a quiet place where you won't be disturbed. Shut the door to outside interference and to the voices that are constantly demanding your attention. Focus on one thing only: this very intimate and private time with the Lord. Time with Him is not just a limited edition; it is a bespoke experience reserved for you exclusively. Let your desire for the Secret Place, the Person of Jesus Christ, be above all else.

FIVE

THE KEY TO THE SECRET PLACE

An infant's perception of colour is not the same as an adult. You can put the same colour in front of an infant and an adult, and although each sees the same colour, it is processed differently in the brain. The adult's brain will process the colour in the part of the brain that deals with language, connecting the perception of colour to concepts it already knows. Whereas the infant's perception of that colour is processed in the pre-linguistic part of the brain. The infant processes colour only as colour and does not perceive or have an awareness of anything other than that.

On the other hand, the adult has a different perception of colour because that perception is connected to knowledge. That creates a different kind of association and level of awareness. This is the key to understanding the Secret Place. Let me explain.

Timing, they say, is everything. But in the spiritual realm, perspective is everything. Your vantage point determines how you interpret and respond to what you see. How do you gain this vantage point? It is through a certain knowledge. The knowledge you have produces a certain awareness, and that awareness dictates how you interpret what you see. This was a lesson learnt by the young man who served Prophet Elisha. In 2 Kings chapter 6, we are given the account. I will provide a brief recap for context.

The king of Syria planned to capture the prophet. So, he sent soldiers in the night to surround the city where the prophet lived. Early the next morning, the young man who served Elisha went out and caught sight of the enemy army. He cried out in terror because all he could see was danger and imminent death. But when Elisha went out and saw what the young man saw, he did not even raise an eyebrow.

How could this be? Both Elisha and the young man were standing in the same physical location, seeing the same thing with their physical eyes. The difference was the young man was only aware of what he could see with his physical eyes. He had no other knowledge. Consequently, he was limited to his physical perspective. Elisha, on the other hand, was seeing things from an entirely different perspective. And from his vantage point, there was no danger whatsoever.

You see, Elisha had esoteric knowledge that gave him a different awareness of his surroundings. As far as the young man could see, the enemy armies with their horses and chariots outnumbered him and his master by the thousands. However, Elisha was aware that the entire mountainside was covered with a vast angelic army. Look at what it says in 2 Kings chapter 6 and verse 16:

2 Kings 6:16

And he [Elisha] answered, Fear not: for they that be with us are more than they that be with them.

When Elisha declared that the angelic army was "more" than the enemy army, he was referring to more than just the number of them. The word that is interpreted as "more" means abounding in quantity, exceedingly greater in size, quality, rank, and strength. The angelic army was superior in every sense of the word.

Because of this awareness, Elisha knew and was confident that the Syrian army was no match for the angelic forces that were backing him up. Although he tried to assure the young man of this reality, Elisha understood that the best way for the young man to be convinced was for him to have the same knowledge. So, Elisha prayed and asked the Lord to open the spiritual eyes of the young man so that he could also see what Elisha saw. And when the young man's eyes were opened, the perception of what he saw changed. He became aware of the place in which he really was, a place of absolute protection.

There are things you can never see until your eyes are opened and you receive revelation. That is why the Bible says, "The entrance of thy words giveth light" (Psalm 119:130). You need to understand that there is a reality that is physical, and a reality that is spiritual. The Secret Place is a spiritual reality, not a physical one. Therefore, you cannot perceive it with your physical faculties. If you try to understand it from a strictly physical perspective, you will miss it entirely. You may have heard people say, "I'm going to the secret place." or "I was in my secret place." They might believe they were, but they are mistaken. The Secret Place is not a location that you can walk into. You can enter at any time, but not physically. You need revelation.

The dilemma of Christians who believe they can physically enter the Secret Place is the same as the infant who sees colour only as colour. They lack esoteric knowledge that would give them the power to perceive beyond what they see physically. They can only interpret what they see through the limited perspective of their flesh. They lack the information that can bring them into the awareness that the Secret Place is a spiritual location and must be understood from a spiritual perspective.

My husband, Prophet Uebert Angel, was taken to Heaven many times in visitations. He has seen incredible wonders, more than you can imagine. He saw mansions in Heaven, entire estates for pastors, prophets, singers, apostles, and others. He was shown those things in the flesh. However, they were not physical mansions. What he identified as physical mansions was his perspective of what he saw from the body. In other words, his earthly body interpreted what he saw as mansions or houses based on the knowledge it had at the time. Now, I want you to follow me closely here because I'm about to show you something extraordinary about the Secret Place that only a few are aware of.

Heaven is a real geographical location in the real estate of the spiritual realm. There are mansions there, but they are not what you think. I want to prove to you how you can misinterpret, or miss altogether, spiritual realities when you associate them with your knowledge of natural things.

Notice what it says in John chapter 14 and verse 2. This is the Lord speaking:

John 14:2

In my Father's house are many mansions: if it were not so, I would have told you. I go to prepare a place for you.

To the spiritually immature, this scripture is not as straightforward as it appears. The inclination would be to interpret it based on your existing knowledge of what a mansion is here on Earth. But herein lies the dilemma: the idea of a house containing many mansions appears to present something of a conundrum. Yet Jesus asserts emphatically that it is indeed so, or He would have told us otherwise. When there is a gap between what you know and what the Bible is saying, the answer is revelation.

I want you to see something very profound here. Most Christians think Jesus is saying He is going to Heaven to prepare physical houses – mansions for us. That is because they have "coloured" what they see in the verse with their own fleshly knowledge of what they understand a "house" or "mansion" to be. Houses on Earth are made of brick and mortar, wood, stone, and whatever other earthly material is used for construction and finishes. But Jesus is not drawing on any earthly reference. He speaks from a place of absolute knowledge and awareness. He is referring to a spiritual place that contains spiritual houses - bodies.

Apostle Paul says it this way in 2 Corinthians chapter 5 and verse 1:

2 Corinthians 5:1

For we know that if our earthly house of *this* tabernacle were dissolved, we have a building of God, an house not made with hands, eternal in the heavens.

We understand that a house is a dwelling place, an inhabited building or one that could be inhabited. But if you stop there, you might miss the revelation and think he is speaking of a physical building. To add clarity to what he is communicating, the apostle goes on to say our earthly house "of this *tabernacle*." Here we begin to get a different understanding of what is being revealed to us.

The word 'tabernacle' is culled from the Greek word *skēnos*. That word does not refer to a house made of brick and mortar; it means *the human body*. Now we can see that the house to which Apostle Paul is referring is the physical body, the one that may feel pain, get tired, age, and die. He is telling you that one day, the earthly body you have will be no more.

The physical body is a seed that is sown. Like all seeds, it will die, or it will be raptured and it will not come back in its original form. The Bible says it this way in 1 Corinthians chapter 15, verses 35 through 38:

1 Corinthians 15:35-38

But some man will say, How are the dead raised up? and with what body do they come? Thou fool, that which thou sowest is not quickened, except it die: And that which thou

sowest, thou sowest not that body that shall be, but bare grain, it may chance of wheat, or of some other grain: But God giveth it a body as it hath pleased him, and to every seed his own body.

When you sow a white maize seed, a green shoot comes out, something completely different from that which was sown. God gives it a body as He pleases and to every seed his own body. Apostle Paul is telling you that your earthly body will be replaced with something completely different from that which was sown. You will have a new, glorious, immortal, indestructible body that is fashioned after Christ's own glorious body. You and I will have a body that is just like His!

It is imperative that you understand the superiority of your spiritual body. So, before I go any further, I want you to pause and think for a moment about your own physical body as it is right now. Whether you realize it or not, that body is a wonder! Let me give you a few facts to prove some of the amazing capabilities of your physical body.

A computer working at 400 million calculations per second, operating for one hundred years, would only accomplish what your brain can accomplish in a single minute. Yes, that brain that you have right now. Additionally, if all the blood vessels of your circulatory system were laid end to end in a line, they would reach about 161,000 kilometres (100,000 miles). To give you an idea of how substantial that is, the Earth's circumference is approximately 25,000 miles. That means the blood vessels inside your body are long enough to wrap around the entire Earth four times.

If that is not astonishing enough, consider this: there is enough DNA in your body to stretch from the Sun to Pluto and back seventeen times! To put that into perspective, the distance from the Earth to the Sun is 150 million kilometres (93.495 million miles). That is a staggering reality when you understand that the distance from the Sun to Pluto is nearly forty times the distance from the Earth to the Sun. If you were travelling at a maximum velocity of 590 miles per hour, it would take you 680 years to make a one-way trip to Pluto one time!

Functioning inside your physical body is a whole world of complex structures with astounding capabilities. If your natural body can contain such sophisticated architecture and immense capacity, how much more your spiritual body?

Right now, you are more than you think you are. And the things I have mentioned are just a fraction of what your physical body is capable of. Now, with those things in mind, consider Jesus and His glorious body. Jesus' body was also sown as a seed. It went down to the grave one way but was raised something far superior. You are in a body, yet it is referred to as your house. Christ also has a body, a glorious house.

In John chapter 14, He said, "I go to prepare a place for you," a mansion not made of brick and mortar, but a glorious house – a spiritual body like unto His own. When you consider that right now you have multiple millions of miles of structures in your physical body, it should not be difficult to comprehend that within the glorious body of Jesus, which is far superior to this earthly body, the capacity and capabilities are immeasurably vast. Our mansions – the glorified spiritual bodies that He prepared –

are in a place, and that place is inside the glorious body of Christ.

Christ is a location. Have you not read in the scriptures where it says that we live and move inside Him?

Acts 17:28

For in him we live, and move, and have our being ...

Just as you have a house, God has a house, and within His house are many glorious houses. You are wondering how can a house be filled with other houses? We have already seen that in spiritual language, God calls your body a house. And even the biological makeup of the human body testifies to the potentiality of God's spiritual house. The human body is made up of nearly 40 trillion cells, biological entities that make up your physical house. And here, God is telling you that in His house – His body – there are many mansions, spiritual bodies.

Look at what Paul said to Timothy:

1 Timothy 3:15

But if I tarry long, that thou mayest know how thou oughtest to behave thyself in the house of God, which is the church of the living God, the pillar and ground of the truth.

Apostle Peter concurs in 1 Peter chapter 2, verse 5:

1 Peter 2:5

Ye also, as lively stones, are built up a spiritual house ...

You are "the house of God, which is the church of the living of God." You are not going to be a house of God. You already are. You are a mansion right now in His house. I said it before, you are more than you think you are. Jesus also is more than you think He is. If we can be clothed with a body that is immortal and glorious, that confronts the frailties of this physical body, how much more His glorious body?

THINGS, PLACES AND REVELATION

When Jesus is preached, the Word comes in the form of things, places, and revelation. Some Sunday school teachings have messed up many Christians because we were only taught about Jesus the man. Those teachings have moved us only to the level of things. When you have not gone deeper into the things of the Spirit, when you hear 'Jesus,' you think only of a person. However, when you get deeper into the revelation of who He is, you understand that He is not only a person but also a place.

Now look at this. You're all familiar with this passage of scripture. We'd like to see what Jesus said as He engaged a woman in Sychar, a Samaritan village. The woman had said,

John 4:20, 21, 23

Our fathers worshiped on this mountain, and you Jews say that in Jerusalem is the place

where one ought to worship." But then, Jesus replied, "... The hour cometh, and now is, when the true worshippers shall worship the Father in spirit and in truth: for the Father seeketh such to worship him."

Why did Jesus say that? It's because in the spirit, they'd experience the presence of God anywhere, and everywhere! That's the Secret Place revelation!

Today, everywhere you go, you carry His presence in you and with you. Now you can better understand the words of the Apostle Paul in Acts 17, verse 28:

"For in him we live, and move, and have our being ...."

We're not apart or separate from Him. We don't seek or look for Him; we're in Him and with Him, and He's in us, with us and about us! Wherever you are, wherever you go, you live and move in Him.

This is different from the Old Testament where people had to go to the right place to offer the right sacrifice; if they didn't go to the right place, it was not accepted. In fact, when they set up a new temple in Samaria, God was angry, because according to His instruction, the temple was only to be in Jerusalem. But in Christ Jesus, we worship God with our spirits at any point and at any location. Hallelujah!

The Secret Place is only a secret to those who have not come into this revelation of who He is. As He gets revealed to you bit by bit, you begin to understand him as a Person and ultimately as the Secret Place. It is not prayer that gets you into the Secret Place. It is revelation. When you come into the revelation of who Jesus is, you understand that you do not have to enter the Secret Place at all. You know with perfect knowledge and have complete awareness that you are already there, Christ in you and you in Him. Let's continue in this vein in the next chapter.

SIX

THE PRESENCE OF THE SECRET PLACE

People are drawn to places, particularly those places where the spiritual and the physical intersect. It is not uncommon for devotees to make pilgrimages to specific locations that have spiritual significance for them. The impetus may be the expectation of the miraculous, the fulfilment of a religious rite, or simply the desire to be in the presence of that which is sacred. Such places are where even the most ordinary person can be transported to the realm of the extraordinary. And they can walk away with an awareness that they did not have before visiting that location.

With ever-evolving technology and device accessibility, we can search for just about any location on this planet and beyond, see vivid photographs of it, and research volumes of related information. We can pull up Google Earth and travel to a location virtually. We even have the option to view from satellite or street level. You could be sitting in your house in London and visit Jerusalem nearly 5,000 kilometres away. Why then would a person need to leave their home and travel thousands of miles just to be in a certain location? It is because some locations carry an atmosphere that is not present everywhere.

The presence of God is everywhere in every location at any time. That is what is meant by the omnipresence of God. There is no place where God is not. In consideration of that reality, the psalmist pondered the question, "Where can I go to run away from your presence?" Does such a place even exist? According to what the psalmist declares in Psalm 139, the answer to that question is a resounding 'No!'

Psalm 139:7-11

Whither shall I go from thy spirit? or whither shall I flee from thy presence? If I ascend up into heaven, thou art there: if I make my bed in hell, behold, thou art there. If I take the wings of the morning, and dwell in the uttermost parts of the sea; Even there shall thy hand lead me, and thy right hand shall hold me. If I say, Surely the darkness shall cover me; even the night shall be light about me.

The presence of God cannot be escaped. Wherever you go, it is there. If you go up to Heaven, it is there. If you travel to the remotest corner of the Earth, His presence will be there when you arrive. If you try to hide under the cloak of darkness, His presence will find you there. Even in Hell, God's presence is there.

God has never been anywhere He is not already. The presence of God is everywhere. However, the Person of God is not everywhere. The manifest presence is where the

Person of God is. And where the Person of God is, an atmosphere is created that is saturated with His presence. That location then becomes the Secret Place. Let me explain further.

The Secret Place is a location where God is manifestly present or where the glory of God dwells. Let's look again at Psalm 91, verse 1:

Psalm 91:1

He that dwelleth in the secret place of the most High shall abide under the shadow of the Almighty.

The "shadow of the Almighty" means the Secret Place is not just a location to which you make a pilgrimage, but a place where the atmosphere of God is saturated. So, when you come to a place where you can interact with the presence, the glory, and the atmosphere of God, that place becomes the Secret Place.

A word from God can take you to a place. In Genesis chapter 12, God spoke to Abraham, and he left in search of a place. However, Abraham went in search of a physical thing, not realizing that the word he received was a revelation of a spiritual place that is meant for us. The Bible said Abraham looked for a city whose builder and maker is God (Hebrews 11:10). Prophet Elijah also received a word from God, which led him to the hollow of a cave. He thought that word led him only to a physical place. But the manifest presence of God showed up, and the cave became a Secret Place.

There are designated places on Earth where the concentrated, manifest presence of God may be found. This atmosphere of God exists in specific locations at specific times. For example, there were times in the Old Testament where the glory of God descended on the Tabernacle of the Congregation. At those times, the Tabernacle became the Secret Place because God, a sacred Being, dwelt there. And when the atmosphere of God tabernacles in a place, it becomes sacred; it becomes the Secret Place.

One example is when God wanted to meet with Moses. He called Moses up to Mount Horeb, and when the glory of God descended upon the mountain, it became the Secret Place. It did not become the Secret Place because of the mountain itself or its location. It became the Secret Place because the mountain had become saturated with, and permeated by, the glory of God.

In Exodus 20:21, the Bible says that Moses approached and stepped into the deep darkness where God was.

Exodus 20:21

And the people stood afar off, and Moses drew near unto the thick darkness *where God was* [emphasis added].

When Moses wanted to interact with that Presence, Horeb became that location. At that specific time, that was the location where the glory of God was manifested. The Secret Place for Moses was the glory of God that saturated him and that environment, but he had to go to Horeb to get to it. Moses could step into the glory on those occasions, but he was not a carrier of it. He could only interact with the glory when it was present and when he was at the location where it was present.

The Secret Place was never about the physical location then, nor is it about the physical location now. It is about the Presence. God is holy. Therefore, everything that pertains to God is sacred. So, the moment you begin to interact with the atmosphere of God, even if it's in a public place, that place becomes the Secret Place. If you can discern that atmosphere, you can commune and interact with the Presence of God.

The manifest presence of God is location sensitive. And when you define the Secret Place in terms of location, it is understood to be the atmosphere of God. Wherever that atmosphere of God dwells, it becomes a distinct location where you can commune with God. But I want to be clear that the location in this context is of significance only because the atmosphere of God is in that location.

The Secret Place as a location where the glory of God dwells functions on the strength of discernment – you recognize that the glory of God is present. You can discern the presence of God in a location. For example, when we are in a service and the glory of God increases, sometimes people are moved to the extent of kneeling and weeping. That moment when the atmosphere is saturated with the presence of God, those who are in that location are in the Secret Place.

In that atmosphere, people weep; they forget about everybody else in the service; some have visions. However, after the service, those same people who were weeping in the manifest Presence of God leave, and that experience is gone. The Secret Place, when understood and interacted with in this way, is a lesser revelation. Why? One reason is that the person has to be physically in the location where the Secret Place or the manifest glory of God is or comes. Another reason this is a lesser revelation is that after they have interacted with the Presence – that glorious atmosphere - they can simply walk away from it.

Just as people can travel or make a pilgrimage to a physical location on Earth where they want to experience a specific atmosphere, in the same way, there are physical locations where the manifest presence of God may be found. One such location is our own prayer mountain. Without question, the atmosphere there is charged with the glory of God. The problem is you have to be there and discern it to experience it.

Therefore, when it comes to our understanding of the Secret Place - what it is and how to function there - knowing that revelation is progressive is crucial. In progressive revelation, there are lesser truths, and there are greater truths. In the revelation of the Secret Place, there are greater truths and lesser truths also. The revelation of the person who believes the Secret Place is a location where the glory of God comes is truth, but it is a lesser truth.

You see, when the Word comes to you, it comes in levels. This is what Jesus was communicating in John chapter 6, verse 63:

John 6:63

… The words that I speak unto you, they are spirit, and they are life.

The Word comes to you initially as things. Jesus said, "the words" or the *things* I speak they are spirit, and they are life. The word translated "and" is the Greek word *kai*, which can also be translated *then*. That being the case, you could read and understand the verse this way:

The words that I speak unto you, they are spirit, then they are life.

That lets you know that there is a progression to revelation. It starts out as words – the *logos* – things written in your Bible. As you get deeper into the Word, you progress from the level of things to the level of revelation. Then you progress from revelation to places. That is the highest form of revelation. The definition of the Secret Place as a location where the manifest presence or glory of God descends upon a place is still on the level of things. At this level, one has to wait for the glory of God, like Moses on Mount Horeb.

Many Christians remain on the things level. Their whole focus is on things, the knowledge of the black, white, and red text they read in their Bible. But things have to move to a point where they become revelation – *spirit*. At this level, you become more aware of the Word. You are not simply quoting the scriptures. Instead, a certain revelation of those scriptures gets into your spirit. However, it is critical to note that when you stay at the level of revelation, you will still never fully realize the fullness of who you are or the revelation of the Secret Place in its totality.

There is a level where the Word is no longer just things or revelation. This is the level that Jesus spoke of where the Word becomes *life*, a location where you live, move, and have your being. When the Word becomes life to you, it is no longer restricted to the mere knowledge of the Word. John chapter 1, verses 1 and 14 says it this way:

John 1:1, 14

In the beginning was the Word ... And the Word was made flesh ...

There is a progression where the revelation of the Word must become flesh. You become the Word, and it becomes you. You are enveloped in the Word, and the Word envelopes you. The known and the knower become one. Brothers and sisters, this is the highest revelation of the Secret Place.

Although there are places dedicated to the Lord, you do not have to wait to visit or be in one of those locations to experience the best God has for you right now. So, thinking you need to pray only in a certain location to experience the Secret Place is immature. And when you say things like *today I was in my secret place*, you are really saying there are times you are there and times when you are not. The Secret Place, at its highest revelation, does not work that way.

Remember, it is not the location that makes a place the Secret Place; it is the manifest presence of God that makes it so. Furthermore, it is erroneous to say you have to pray in a certain location to be in the Secret Place. When you say such things, not only are you living beneath your privileges as a New Covenant Christian, but you are also implying that God is limited and can only function when confined to a certain location. In doing so, you relegate the Secret Place to the status of idols that must be stationed in shrines or propped up in corners and visited for the performance of religious rites.

God expects you to advance from the level of things to revelation, and ultimately, to realize that Christ Himself is the Secret Place. Psalm 91, verse 1 speaks of he who dwells in the Secret Place, not he who visits. God's desire is for you to experience the Secret Place as a habitation, not a visitation. You no longer have to wait for the glory of God to come and go like the saints of old. Instead, the Secret Place can become a constant in your life. And in the remaining chapters, I will show you how.

SEVEN

THE POSSIBILITIES OF THE SECRET PLACE

It is impossible for you to think of anything that is impossible. If you can conceive something in your mind, it is possible. Your imaginative ability is the ability of God in you to tap into realms of possibilities that you have not yet seen or experienced physically. This is a universal spiritual endowment that even children utilize. That is why they can play with imaginary friends or visit places they've never been physically. Those friends or places are realities in a spiritual location called their minds. Children easily conceive such things because they lack the rational prejudices of adulthood that tell them they cannot or should not do otherwise. Therefore, they freely engage in that spiritual realm at will.

Thoughts themselves are things that exist in the spiritual realm. They are spiritual realities. You may not see them or be able to touch them physically, yet you can enter the thought realm and interact with realities that exist there. And in that location in your mind, the impossible becomes possible. Furthermore, just as it is not possible for you to think of anything impossible, it is also impossible to think of something that does not already exist. Let me give you a quick mental exercise to prove the point.

I want you to imagine an animal that you have never seen before. There is only one condition: it cannot look like anything you've ever seen or heard of. I'll wait. In fact, if you can do it, I'll give you a briefcase of money. You cannot do it. Why? Because with your natural mind, you cannot think of something that exists outside of the realm of your present reality. The fact that you can conceive something in your mind is proof that it exists.

Now, my reality may be vastly different from yours because my exposure and experiences may differ from what you have experienced. If that were true, that would mean there are realities I can tap into that you may not have accessed or been exposed to yet. But what if there was a way for you to tap into realities that are in my mind? Better yet, what if you were able to think the thoughts of the most superior mind in the universe? You are wondering how that could be possible. It is possible, and it is one of many advantages of being in the Secret Place.

In the previous chapter, we discussed the Secret Place as the atmosphere of God that comes to a location. At such times, if you can discern that atmosphere, you have the privilege of interacting with the manifest presence of God. That, however, is a revelation of the Secret Place at a junior level. There is another level of revelation superior to that. Instead of waiting for the Secret Place to come to you, you can go to it, stay there and partake of the realities that exist there.

At this level of revelation, the Secret Place is no longer only a place where the Presence of God is manifested. The Secret Place at this level of understanding is a location in Christ where you access divine realities. However, that does not mean that it is a singular location in Christ. There are many locations in Christ, not just one.

Many Christians have not caught the fulness of the revelation that the Person of Christ contains places, and those places are accessible to those who are in Christ. Yet the Bible clearly states that it is so. Notice what the scripture says in Ephesians chapter 1 and verse 3:

Ephesians 1:3

Blessed be the God and Father of our Lord Jesus Christ, who hath blessed us with all spiritual blessings in heavenly places in Christ.

God has blessed every Christian with all spiritual blessings *in heavenly places*. That does not mean that your blessings are scattered like seeds in various parts of Heaven. Nor do you have to guess where your blessings are. The verse tells you precisely where they are. They are in heavenly places, and those heavenly places are *in Christ Jesus*. And whenever you access any spiritual blessing, you are in the Secret Place.

The scripture leaves no room for dispute. Clearly, there are *places* in Christ Jesus. So when we refer to the Secret Place, as understood at this second level revelation, we are referring to *locations* in Christ Jesus where the realities of God dwell. That is why Jesus declared, "**I am the way,**

the truth, and the life." (John 14:6). You can only access these realities through Christ (the Way). He is the revelation (the Truth) and the substance of those realities (the Life). Why? Because He is the Secret Place in which these realities reside.

These realities are substantiated in Christ. When you step into those realities, you are interacting with them from a physical location. At the same time, you are in Christ. So, the Secret Place at this level of revelation is not just a location where the glory has come, but it is where you are in Christ at any given time.

You can actually identify where you are as a Christian by your level of understanding of the Secret Place. Are you still functioning at the level of things, waiting for the Presence of God to visit a location? Or have you graduated to understanding the Secret Place as revelation that gives you access to locations – spiritual realities – in Christ?

The Holy Spirit is the tour guide that brings you to these locations through revelation. He is the One who reveals to you the spiritual realities located in Christ. Apostle Paul says it this way in 1 Corinthians chapter 2 and verse 7:

1 Corinthians 2:7

But we speak the wisdom of God in a mystery, even the hidden wisdom, which God ordained before the world unto our glory.

Apostle Paul was not functioning at this secondary level of revelation. However, by the Spirit of God, he understood the necessity of making us aware that there are locations in

Christ that can be accessed through revelation. He says we speak the wisdom of God in a "mystery." That word 'mystery' is translated from the Greek word *mystérion*, which means something that is entered by those with revelation.

The wisdom of God is a spiritual reality. Access to this wisdom is not restricted to apostles, prophets, pastors, or teachers only. It is restricted to those who have been given revelation, and that is possible for every Christian. Also, I want you to notice the definite article that is used in Apostle Paul's construct of the verse we read. He says, "even *the* hidden wisdom." He is referring to a specific kind of wisdom that is hidden and can only be found in one location. That location is the Secret Place.

The Secret Place is a Person – the Lord Jesus Christ – and in Him, there are locations we can access by revelation. Apostle Paul says it this way in Colossians chapter 2, verse 3:

Colossians 2:3

In whom are hid all the treasures of wisdom and knowledge.

Wisdom is one of the many locations in Christ. Knowledge is another. These are spiritual realities that are hidden in the Secret Place. And as we go a little further into the passage from 1 Corinthians chapter 2, we will see how crucial and integral the involvement of the Holy Spirit is in our discovery of these locations. Look at verses 9 and 10:

1 Corinthians 2:9-10

But as it is written, Eye hath not seen, nor ear heard, neither have entered into the heart of man, the things which God hath prepared for them that love him. But God hath revealed them unto us by his Spirit: for the Spirit searcheth all things, yea, the deep things of God.

Without the Holy Spirit, you cannot access these locations. It would be like trying to imagine something that does not look like anything you've ever seen or heard of before. You cannot see, hear, or imagine these spiritual realities unless the Holy Spirit reveals them to you.

Revelation can come to you at any given time. You can be reading your Bible or listening to a message being preached, and revelation comes to you. Or you can be in prayer, and suddenly the wisdom of God is revealed to you. You have entered a location in the Secret Place (Christ) where wisdom is found. You have migrated from the terrestrial to the celestial, from the mundane to the sacred. You are not necessarily in a place per se; to be more precise, you are in a reality that is captured within Christ.

Earlier I asked the question, *what if you could think the thoughts of the most superior mind in the universe?* If that were possible, you could tap into realities you do not have access to with your natural mind. I can assure you, it is possible, but only in the Secret Place. The Bible says it this way in 1 Corinthians chapter 2, verse 16:

1 Corinthians 2:16

**For who hath known the mind of the Lord,
that he may instruct him?** *But we have the
mind of Christ* **[emphasis added].**

The mind of Christ is one of the locations in the Secret
Place. You have perpetual access, not only when you receive
your glorified body, but right this minute. That means it is
possible for you to tap into the consciousness of God and
access divine realities.

This is privileged access at the highest degree, because the
mind of Christ contains an immeasurable and unlimited
store of divine realities. Entire worlds are created out of that
location. We see this in Hebrews 11, verse 3:

Hebrews 11:3

**Through faith we understand that the worlds
were framed by the word of God, so that
things which are seen were not made of
things which do appear.**

The *worlds* were framed by the Word of God! That is an
extraordinary truth. You may not catch this revelation until
I explain God's creative process. Follow closely on this next
point so that you don't miss your access to this dimension of
the Secret Place.

Most Christians are familiar with Genesis chapter 1, verse
1, which gives us an account of the beginning of creation. I
want us to focus on the first part of verse 1:

Genesis 1:1

In the beginning God created ...

Now, when you look at the word "created," you might be tempted to think that God just stepped on the scene and immediately started making things out of thin air. However, His creative process was a bit more involved than that. According to the verse we read in Hebrews 11:3, we understand that He spoke everything into existence. However, His creative process did not start in His mouth; it started in His mind.

When God wanted to create, He first engaged His imagination to form the things He desired in His mind. He then spoke those things into existence. The Bible says that the Holy Ghost brooded in constant imagination of the things to be created. *Then* God spoke.

Genesis 1:2b-3a

And the Spirit of God moved [*brooded in constant imagination of a thing,* emphasis added] upon the face of the waters. And God said, Let there be ...

With that understanding in mind, let us return to Hebrews 11:3:

Hebrews 11:3

Through faith we understand that the worlds were framed by the word of God, so that things which are seen were not made of things which do appear.

The worlds were *framed* as part of God's creative process. How? The same way it was stated in Genesis 1, verse 2 – in the mind or imagination of God. In fact, to imagine a thing literally means to frame it in the mind. So, the worlds that God created existed first in the location in heavenly places known as the mind of Christ. His mind is a location in the Secret Place. And because you have the mind of Christ, access to that location is granted to you now. That means you can understand, reason, think, and imagine just as He does, not after the rapture, but right now.

Jesus made the worlds by framing them in his mind. That means they existed in His mind before they were ever spoken into physical manifestation. Just imagine the thoughts you could have as you tap into the reality of the mind of Christ, not when you receive your glorious body, but right now! Then, you would understand why Jesus said nothing shall be impossible to you (see Matthew 17:20).

This revelation of the Secret Place as the location of spiritual realities in Christ is accessed by faith. That means you can decide to enter at any time. Faith itself is also a location in the Secret Place that you entered at the moment of salvation. Faith is a reality that God fully expects you to live in right now in your day-to-day life. Look at what the Word of God says in Galatians chapter 2, verse 20:

Galatians 2:20

I am crucified with Christ: nevertheless I live; yet not I, but Christ liveth in me: and the life which I now live in the flesh *I live by the faith of the Son of God* [emphasis added], who loved me, and gave himself for me.

The King James Version translates the emphasized phrase as "I live by the faith *of* the Son of God." But the literal translation is "I live by faith *in* the Son of God." Faith is a spiritual reality that exists *in* Christ, the Secret Place.

We no longer need to live a life predicated on the dictates or vulnerabilities of flesh and blood. We live by the faith that is *in* the Son of God. Anything that could negatively affect your physical body or contaminate your blood or bloodlines cannot touch you when you grasp the revelation of the Secret Place. Life in the Secret Place is the life God wants for every Christian.

As the revelation of the Secret Place dawns on your spirit, you understand that your life is no longer subject to the limitations of mere men. You are more than a human being. And it is God's desire that you live a supernatural life from the realm of the Secret Place. It is the higher life!

As we bring this particular point of discussion to a close, it is essential to understand that Christ is a system. Christ is governmental. Mansions exist in Him. Spiritual realities exist in Him. Dimensions of those realities exist in Him. In fact, all things exist in Him. Ephesians 1, verse 10 says it this way:

Ephesians 1:10

That in the dispensation of the fulness of times he might gather together in one all things in Christ, both which are in heaven, and which are on earth; even in him.

Understanding that all things are in Christ means, as a Christian, you can be functioning in a certain dimension of the Secret Place at any given moment. This is not about God coming into a physical location such as a prayer room, mountain, or church building. This is about you coming into a location in God through revelation. As long as you are functioning by the protocol of that revelation, you are in the Secret Place. If you do not catch the revelation of the Secret Place, you will never fully benefit from being a Christian. There must be an awakening to this reality, and that is taking place even as you read the words on this page.

You no longer have to be someone who waits to discern and interact with the atmosphere of God when it comes. You can be one of the enlightened few who does not have to wait for the glory of God to saturate a place. At any time, you can decide to step into that glorious atmosphere of the Secret Place by faith as revelation comes to you. Right now, you are being called to a dimension where you go beyond discerning the atmosphere of God to carrying the atmosphere of God. You are answering a call to rise up into higher dimensions in the Secret Place.

Remember, you enter the Secret Place by revelation, and that revelation is progressive. The first level of revelation of the Secret Place is that the manifest presence of God comes into a physical location where you can interact with it there. The glory comes down to where you are. At this next level of revelation of the Secret Place, you are caught up into the celestial realms, accessing spiritual realities in Christ through revelation that is given to you. But there is something greater, the ultimate level in this progressive revelation that will take you to a dimension of the Secret Place where you function exactly as God does.

It might seem inconceivable to you right now that you have the capacity to function as God does, create as He creates, and bring spiritual realities into existence in the physical realm right here and right now. You would not be the first to struggle with this reality of the Secret Place. The Old Testament is replete with examples of those who initially could not conceive their capabilities until they were drawn into the Secret Place by God Himself. We will examine a couple of these examples in the next chapter as we go deeper into the highest revelation of the Secret Place.

EIGHT

THE PROBLEM WITH THE SECRET PLACE

In 1989, a thirteen-year-old boy from St. Croix had big dreams of becoming an Olympic swimmer. His mother, recognizing his love of swimming and his raw talent, enrolled him in competitive swimming. She was his number one encourager, shuttling him back and forth to train at the only Olympic-sized pool on the island and fuelling his dreams with her favourite poolside mantra.

However, on September 20th of that year, his dreams were all but shattered. Hurricane Hugo pummelled the island, destroying eighty-five per cent of the buildings, including the pool where he trained. Seven months later, tragedy struck again, and a day before his fourteenth birthday, his mother passed away. Devastated by her passing, the young teen gave up on his Olympic dreams. The pool reminded him too much of his mother.

Eventually, he pursued a different sport, basketball. In time, he went on to become part of the greatest class of basketball players to ever grace the sport. And some thirty-one years after his mother's passing, Tim Duncan, the boy from St.

Croix, was inducted into the Naismith Basketball Hall of Fame as one of the greatest of all time. In an emotional speech that left few dry eyes in the room, he quoted his beloved mother's poolside mantra: "Good, better, best. Never let it rest until your good is better, and your better is best."

In the revelation of the Secret Place, there is good, better, and best. Discerning the atmosphere of God is good. Stepping into spiritual realities in Christ is better. But you can never be a full-fledged Christian growing spiritually without understanding the Secret Place as complete and total oneness with the Person of Jesus Christ. That is God's best for you.

The accurate revelation of the Secret Place is a Person – the Person of Christ. And the highest purpose of the Secret Place is to attain the mystery of oneness. From the beginning, God had nothing less than oneness with Him on His mind. His desire was for God and man to become one, existing as co-heirs of the purposes of God. That is His ultimate intention. However, there is one thing standing in your way, something you are battling to control every day, perhaps without even knowing it. And that is your soul.

The complications of the soul cause problems in a Christian's life. If you do not understand the soul, how it works, and how to control it, you can never understand the Secret Place in its fullness and live a life of oneness with Christ. Therefore, it is of the utmost importance that we comprehend this strange entity we call the soul. Many Christians are taught and believe that God created the soul when He created man. However, this is a false belief. God did not create the soul. To understand the soul and its original state of being, we must go back to the beginning – Genesis.

In the beginning, the mind of God was engrossed with the thought of creating something that did not exist before. He wanted something that was like Him, not only in resemblance and in representation, but something that also functioned in His will and in the totality of who He is. His desire was to create something that was relational to Him. In other words, God wanted a creation that walks like Him, talks like Him, whose thought processes and mindset were exactly the same as His own.

From our earliest years in Sunday School, we are taught that God formed man from the dirt and breathed the breath of life into his nostrils. However, there was a part of the creative process of man with which God had nothing to do. As shocking as that sounds, it is actually stated in Genesis chapter 2 and verse 7, a key verse in your understanding of the Secret Place.

Genesis 2:7

And the Lord God formed man of the dust of the ground, and breathed into his nostrils the breath of life; and man became a living soul.

Remember, as we discussed in the previous chapter, God created the world in His mind, and then He made it. Now, here in Genesis 2, verse 7, the Bible tells us that God formed the man of the dust of the ground. We need to understand that God is a spiritual being, and up until this point, His experiences were spiritual. But now, as He forms man, He is interacting and having an experience with something physical – He scooped up dust from the ground and formed a man.

Before I go any further, it is important to note that it is impossible for anything to come out of God – His mind, His words, His being – that is not perfect. Therefore, there is nothing He has created that is not perfect. So, when God created man, He created two perfect things: a perfect spirit and a perfect body.

Remember, God is looking to create something that has never been seen before, something superior to anything He has ever done up to this point. And so, when we look at this scripture, it says God formed man out of the dust of the ground and breathed into his nostrils the breath of life. But then something strange happened. There was an intercourse, an intertwining, that took place between spirit and body, which gave birth to something completely new, something with which God Himself had no experience. When the breath of life, which became man's spirit, came into contact with his body, it produced the soul.

Now, we understand that God is all-knowing. That is why He is called the omniscient God; He knows the A to Z of everything. But that speaks of His spiritual knowledge or knowing something spiritually as a Spirit being. God knew spiritually that when He brought the spirit and the body together, something would happen. Yet, it was something that He had not seen or experienced physically. Adam was unlike anything that had ever been created on this planet. And part of what makes him such a unique creation is this new entity that came into being, a progeny of the spirit and the body called the soul.

So, we have established that the soul is an offspring of two perfect things, man's spirit and body. It is a by-product of the intermingling of the spirit and the body. And so, we have the spirit, which was created, and we have the flesh, which was also created. But then we have the soul, which is a mixture of the two, a fusion of the two created things. But the soul was not created by God. The Bible says, "man *became* a living soul." The soul was not created; it became.

You are wondering, *what does all this have to do with the Secret Place?* It has everything to do with the Secret Place. As I said earlier, if you do not understand how the soul came into being and how it works, you can never enter into the fulness of the revelation of the Secret Place. So, let us continue our discourse about this peculiar progeny called the soul.

Let me reiterate: the soul was not created by God; it became. It was the coming together of two pure elements to create something that was unique. The flesh and the spirit are God's workmanship. But now, we are seeing this thing that is not directly linked to God's workmanship. So, we have the spirit, the body, and then the soul. These are three elements, two of which have been created by God personally. He creates a perfect spirit and a perfect body, then the soul becomes an intermingling of these two perfect elements.

That means your soul is half spirit, half flesh, a combination of two different types of being. This mixture of perfect and imperfect is precisely what causes complications in the life of a Christian. Like a mixed-race child, the soul can have identity issues; it struggles to know where it belongs. Is it fleshly or is it spiritual?

It is very important that you understand that the body was created perfect and pure by God. You see, His ultimate intention has always been to live in your body, to make it His headquarters. Therefore, it had to be something that was created pure. But herein lies the dilemma. The body is created to be perfect, yet the flesh can be sinful; it can be sick; it can be broke. So, how is it that God created something so perfect, yet it has become so flawed? It is because of the soul.

The soul lacks the purity of the spirit and the body because it is not created by God. So these two perfect entities struggle for control over this brand new imperfect entity that came into being. Galatians chapter 5, verse 17 says it this way:

Galatians 5:17

For the flesh lusteth against the Spirit, and the Spirit against the flesh: and these are contrary the one to the other: so that ye cannot do the things that ye would.

What does the Bible mean when it says the flesh and the spirit "lusteth against" each other? It simply means that in the life of a Christian, the flesh has a strong desire that goes against what the Spirit wants. Conversely, what the Spirit wants goes against what the flesh wants. They are contrary or opposed to one another, each fighting for control of the soul. You, however, are the one who determines who the winner will be.

You see, whatever you exercise yourself towards determines whether your soul will be controlled by the flesh or by the

Spirit. If you are more inclined to the things of the Spirit, your soul will lean more in that direction. But if you are more prone to the things of the world and the flesh, that's exactly where your soul will lean. Your soul simply submits to the one that wins the fight. And if your soul is won over by the flesh, you cannot understand the revelation of the Secret Place.

This soulish struggle is not anything new. From the beginning of time, men and women have fought the battle over the soul. Many times they've lost the battle. There were generals in the Old Testament, great men and women of God, that were used mightily under the unction of the Spirit of God. Yet many of them struggled to enter the Secret Place because of issues of the soul. While there were many, we will look at two of them: Gideon and Moses.

Gideon is recorded in the Bible's celebrity hall of fame for his remarkable feats. In Judges chapter 7, the Bible records how Gideon defeated an entire host of the Midianite army with only three hundred men. Even in the New Testament, Gideon is one of the notable giants of faith recorded in Hebrews chapter 11, verses 32 to 34, which says:

Hebrews 11:32-34

And what shall I more say? for the time would fail me to tell of Gedeon, and of Barak, and of Samson, and of Jephthae; of David also, and Samuel, and of the prophets: Who through faith subdued kingdoms, wrought righteousness, obtained promises, stopped the mouths of lions. Quenched the violence of fire, escaped the edge of the sword, out of

weakness were made strong, waxed valiant in fight, turned to flight the armies of the aliens.

Gideon here is named among some of the most valiant men in the Bible. But before his revelation of the Secret Place, he was full of fear and had major self-esteem issues.

We find him in Judges chapter 6, verse 11, threshing wheat in a winepress.

Judges 6:11

And there came an angel of the Lord, and sat under an oak which was in Ophrah, that pertained unto Joash the Abiezrite: and his son Gideon threshed wheat by the winepress, to hide it from the Midianites.

Just in case you did not know, wheat is typically threshed in a large open area called a threshing floor. Whereas winepresses are smaller, usually enclosed, areas for crushing grapes. But Gideon is so fearful that he threshes wheat in the winepress so he can hide from the Midianites. I want you to see what can happen when the soul grapples with the revelation of the Secret Place.

We see in verse 11 that an Angel of the Lord appears to Gideon right there in his hiding place. But I want you to notice how the Angel greets Gideon in verse 12:

Judges 6:12

> **And the angel of the Lord appeared unto him,
> and said unto him, The Lord is with thee,
> thou mighty man of valour.**

Wait a minute! How is this Angel greeting this fearful man as a "mighty man of valour?" The man is hiding! What is so mighty about that? Gideon is greeted this way because a revelation is taking place. Notice what the Angel says first: "The Lord is with thee." That's a revelation of the Secret Place. But as you can imagine, Gideon doesn't get it right away.

First, he starts out blame-shifting, accusing God of abandoning His people and leaving them to suffer under the hands of their enemies. Gideon is yet to learn that the Secret Place is oblivious to complaints. The Angel continues in verse 14:

> **Judges 6:14**
>
> **And the Lord looked upon him, and said, Go
> in this thy might, and thou shalt save Israel
> from the hand of the Midianites: have not I
> sent thee?**

The Angel is showing Gideon the reality of who he is in the Secret Place, but Gideon, like so many Christians today, is still not getting it. He moves from complaining to pouring out one excuse after another. *How can I save Israel? I'm poor. I come from the poorest family in our tribe. Not only that, but I am the youngest and least significant member of my family.* But once again, the Angel shows Gideon a revelation of the Secret Place. Look at what it says in verse 16:

Judges 6:16

And the Lord said unto him, Surely I will be with thee, and thou shalt smite the Midianites as one man.

Again, the Lord reassures Gideon that His Presence is with him and strengthens His affirmation of Gideon's abilities in the Secret Place. He tells Gideon in effect, as long as My presence is with you, you can smite an entire army on your own.

Do you realize that if Gideon had not doubted his own capacity, the man was literally going to go *singlehandedly* against at least 135,000 soldiers and win! That is a glimpse of the power of the Secret Place once that revelation gets into your spirit. Still, Gideon continues to struggle in his soul. He graduates from making excuses to doubting who is even talking to him. He even goes as far as to ask the Lord to show proof of identification. After getting the confirmation he requested, finally convinced of the revelation he received, Gideon goes on to do exploits.

The most striking thing is how the Lord approaches an ordinary man and tells him something unfamiliar that contradicts everything about his life and surroundings. The Lord ignores every excuse and affirms a reality that confronts and directly opposes the way the man sees himself. Furthermore, He fully expects Gideon to act on what He has said based on one thing: Gideon has just received a revelation of the Secret Place.

The reason Gideon doubted was he did not know that he had a Secret Place in him. Therefore, he was not aware of his capabilities there. But an awakening took place after realizing the Presence of the Lord was indeed with him. Something awakened inside Gideon, and he finally realized who he truly was and lived up to it. He was, without a doubt, a mighty man of valour. But it took a revelation of the Secret Place, through the Word of God, for Gideon to overcome the struggle in his soul and begin to see himself that way.

Another example is Moses, a man of great renown who came to be known as the friend of God. Whenever we talk about the Hall of Fame of Christianity, we never cease to mention Moses. This man became the instrument of emancipation for millions of enslaved people. He released plagues on command, and he even parted the Red Sea so that the Children of Israel could walk to freedom on dry land. The man is so famous, even Hollywood has cashed in on his popularity. But if we were to do a background check on this extraordinary champion of God, before we came to know him as such, we would see that Moses fought and lost the battle of his soul on more than one occasion.

You see, before Moses became the friend of God, he was a man who lacked confidence and even opposed God. In fact, when you read through Exodus chapters 3 and 4, it is evident that the flesh was dominating Moses' soul. He had an incredible encounter with the manifest presence of God that would convince the staunchest atheist. But even in the midst of that astounding personal encounter, Moses still struggled to see himself as God saw him.

Moses had extremely low self-esteem, due in part to his speech impediment. Moreover, he was a man on the run, a fugitive who was familiar with fear. His soul was dominated by these issues. So much so, even when God Himself assured him that His presence, power, and protection would be with him, Moses would not be convinced. He just could not imagine he was chosen to be the deliverer of God's people.

He raised one objection after the other, arguing with God. *They won't trust me. They won't listen to a word I say. They're going to say, of all people, why would God did talk to you? I don't talk well. I've never been good with words, neither before nor after You spoke to me. I stutter and stammer. Please, send somebody else!* Moses' flesh had thoroughly convinced his soul that he was unqualified, incompetent, and ill-equipped to do what God said he had the power to do. This conflict of soul initially caused him to miss the revelation of the Secret Place. If it were not for the mercy of God, Moses would have missed it altogether.

But the Bible celebrity we now know as Moses is not the confidence-lacking excuse-making Moses that stood before the burning bush. Somewhere between doubter and deliverer, stammerer and God's spokesman, he awakened to the reality of the Secret Place. He caught the revelation of who he was in God, and with that revelation, not even the Red Sea could stand in His way.

Moses and Gideon were each called into a certain revelation of the Secret Place. And in so doing, they were uprooted from the mediocre and mundane and thrust into lives of adventure and total victory, lives marked by the supernatural power and presence of God. They were never told to enter a room. Neither were they told to walk through a door or go to a mountain. Instead, they were given a revelation of the Secret Place. And that revelation is the one that they believed and applied, and it worked for them.

I am here to tell you that you are better than Gideon and Moses. As a New Covenant Christian, you have the greatest advantage, one that none of the Old Testament believers had. Not even Adam in the Garden of Eden had this advantage. Remember that Adam was formed from the dust of the ground by God, a perfect body. And God breathed into his nostrils the breath of life, creating a perfect spirit. But the soul of Adam became an imperfect, impure entity, struggling to know where to belong. This was true of Adam and of every person who is not born again. But it is not true of you, the New Covenant Christian. You are superior to Adam.

You see, God's original agenda never changed. He still wants you to be just like Him. He created you to host His presence. And like Him, He created you with the ability to interact with the physical yet be impervious to it. He created you a new species of being that never existed before. But this time, He did not form you from the dust of the ground; He scooped you out of His own glorious flesh, the Lord Jesus Christ. He did not breathe into your nostrils the breath of life. Instead, he did something much better. He, who is Spirit, stepped inside your being! There was an intermingling, an intertwining of His Spirit and your recreated spirit, that created something pure, perfect, and powerful!

Your only problem is you have spent your B.C. (before Christ) years (and perhaps some after) feeding your flesh with information from the world and believing things that cause the soul to lean towards mindsets of failure, depravity, loss, and lack. These things, like an electric fence, stop you from entering into the revelation of the Secret Place and keep you on the periphery of God's best for you. That is why it is vital for you to renew your mind with God's word.

The Bible says that you must be "transformed by the renewing of your mind" (see Romans 12:2). This is not the kind of transformation that comes as a result of changes you make physically. Acting and speaking like a Christian contribute to that transformation, but the major change is taking place in the soul. Whatever you start saying registers in your soul, in your mindset. And whatever starts registering in your soul then becomes what your body is saying.

How many times have you confessed something, yet every single day, it is the direct opposite of what you said? It seems like the more you say one thing, a whole other thing shows up in your life. Why is that? It is because there is a disconnect that has taken place in the soul, which lies at the intersection of your recreated spirit and your flesh. There is something there that needs to be transformed from the inside. This is why we always talk about a change that takes place from the inside out. We are referring to a transformation that is taking place within your soul. And then that transformation affects your body, and it also affects your spirit.

So, the complications of the soul cause problems in a Christian's life, and they cause you not to understand what the Secret Place truly is. And this is why many people think the Secret Place must be in a cupboard somewhere, or on a mountain, or they create a "secret place" in a room in their house. Such error comes as a result of complications created in the soul, complications of not understanding the Word, complications of not understanding revelation.

Any Christian you ever hear saying, I need to sing in order to get into the Secret Place, or I need to fast to enter the Secret Place, or who thinks the Secret Place is something that they need to get into, is a person whose soul is leaning more towards the flesh than the spirit. There are worship leaders all over the world that say things like, "Raise your hands, right now. We are about to enter the Secret Place." That is what happens when you don't understand the revelation of it.

The only way you can enter the Secret Place is if your mind is renewed. That only happens as you give yourself over to the Word and allow it to prevail over your soul. Acts 19, verse 12 says it this way:

Acts 19:12

So mightily grew the word of God and prevailed.

The Word in you will prevail over the mindset of the world and the flesh and turn your soul over to the control of the Spirit where it belongs. Instead of spending the whole night scrolling on social media platforms that do nothing for you, study the Word. You are delving into the Word, looking at it and wanting to understand it because you now know that the Secret Place is not really a physical place but a Person with whom you share intimate oneness.

That is the highest revelation of the Secret Place. It is not just about the presence of God that you interact with in a location, or a location where you access spiritual realities in Christ. The highest comprehension of the Secret Place becomes a matter of consciousness and intimacy, a constant awareness that you are one with Christ. First Corinthians 6, verse 17 says it this way:

1 Corinthians 6:17

But he that is joined unto the Lord is one spirit.

The Secret Place is our oneness with God through Jesus Christ. That is the core of it. The reason it is called a secret is that we cannot perceive it with our natural senses. It can only be known by revelation. Yet it is the most real "place" imaginable.

Brothers and sisters, the life of Christ in us is another kind of life, incomparable to the one we were born with through natural birth. It is a life that is not of the flesh. When Christ comes to dwell in us, we become one with Him in Spirit – our human spirit is supplanted by the Spirit of life. This oneness is the Secret Place of the Most High. It is His abode in us and our abode in Him. It is Christ in you, the hope of glory!

This is what God wanted all along – no distinction between you and Him, only absolute oneness. He wants you to live with such an awareness of Christ in you and you in Christ that when you're walking down the street and someone says "Jesus," you answer! In this revelation of the Secret Place, there is no differentiation between you and Christ; no one can tell where you end and where Christ starts. You are one, inseparable, indistinguishable, and walking in oneness with Christ because you are joined with the Lord.

When you catch this revelation that the Secret Place is a Person, and that Person is Christ in you, then you understand that you carry the Secret Place everywhere you go. As long as that consciousness is alive in you, you are dwelling in the Secret Place. That means you can be walking through the airport, shopping in the market, wherever doing whatever, and still be interacting with the fullness of God. You have left the subject of location. You are now dealing with a personality. So, it is intimacy; it is oneness. This is the highest realm of interaction where you become like your God. You realize that sickness, poverty, and lack should not even be a part of your life because the Secret Place has taken up residence – indefinite leave to remain – on the inside of you.

One thing is certain, when you understand that you are in the Secret Place, there is nothing that you cannot do. There is nothing you cannot say. God told Moses I will be with your mouth. But you are better than Moses. You are one with Christ, flesh of His flesh and bone of His bones. He is not *with* your mouth. In the Secret Place, you understand that when you speak, Christ is speaking. In the Secret Place, He is not leading you anywhere. No! When you walk, that's Christ walking. When you reach out your hand to heal the sick, that's Christ's hand touching that person. When you wake up in the morning, you wake up in the Secret Place. What news could possibly trouble you there?

Imagine rising from your bed and telling yourself, nothing is impossible with me today! There is no room for sickness or lack when the Secret Place is in you. By the revelation of and participation with the Secret Place, how can your business ever fail? Your soul never has to struggle or be inundated by the cares of this life. They simply do not exist in the Secret Place.

When you are in the Secret Place and understand that the Secret Place is alive in you, you will declare:

> **Christ with me. Christ before me. Christ behind me. Christ in me. Christ beneath me. Christ above me. Christ on my right. Christ on my left. Christ when I lie down. Christ when I sit down. Christ when I arise.**

The Secret Place is living on the inside of you! He is a part of you. He is a part of everything that you do. This is the highest revelation of the Secret Place, an abiding and constant consciousness that Christ is in you. You are fully aware, participating with what is known. You no longer say, with God nothing is impossible. No, not with God; with *me*, nothing is impossible!

Your soul is like a sponge. It will simply absorb more and more from whichever direction you push it towards. It is designed to absorb, whether from the spirit or from the flesh. All it does is stay there and absorb from these two beings that were created by the Lord. Remember, the soul became, and so it cannot be perfect. You are the one who is perfect in Christ.

And so, when you fill your days with the Word, talking the Word, living your life centred in and around the Word, you are training your soul. Your soul has to awaken to this revelation. And the more you awaken to this reality, the more your body starts to listen. Everything that becomes real in the capacity of your soul, everything you say, will surely come to pass. It does not matter how big or ridiculous it sounds. If you say, "I shall prosper," then you shall prosper. It does not matter what report you got from the doctor or what the x-ray says; that body has no choice but to listen. This is because you are speaking from the Secret Place, from the position of Christ in you, dwelling in you. You have made Him your own habitation.

In the Secret Place, you are communing together with the Lord. Your soul is in sync with your spirit and not your flesh. In the Secret Place, your soul is not ruled by your flesh; it is ruled by your spirit. And ultimately, anything your spirit says from this position of oneness is coming from God. If He says, you are a mighty man or woman of valour, or you can defeat any army, you catch it and bring it to the faculty of your soul. Your soul then has to align everything in your body. Your flesh will have no choice.

You are the one who determines who is going to be master over your flesh. Consequently, you decide who rules over your soul. The optimal positioning of your soul is up to you. Go for the best. It has been said that the enemy of great is good, so don't stop where you are. Don't stop at an atmosphere or intermittent accessing of spiritual realities. Go for the ultimate revelation of oneness with God. Never let it rest until your good is better, and your better is best.

NINE

THE POWER OF THE SECRET PLACE

My favourite place to be in the whole world is in a bulldozer. I know you were expecting me to say The Seychelles or somewhere exotic. Being in the construction business, I've had a go at a bulldozer or two. My favourite being a 183 tonne, 1,350 horsepower, 12-meter-long bulldozer. A bulldozer removes impossibilities. It can clear any obstacle in your way. You can bulldoze a whole mountain, clear an entire forest, or flatten a building in a matter of minutes. You do not need to exert your own strength. Once you are inside a bulldozer, it transfers its power and capabilities to you, making you an unstoppable force to be reckoned with.

When you are in the Secret Place, you are in the Supernatural Bulldozer called Jesus Christ. You are inside Him, and He is inside you. You are an irresistible force; you laugh at "impossible," you move forward with unstoppable power, and you crush any obstacle that dares to confront you. You are in a Place that is better than the most powerful super dozers on this planet, a Place where poverty is pulverized, and every form of lack is eradicated. You are in a Place that makes you invulnerable to sickness and diseases. No matter the variant or the stage, you reside in the Secret Place, a place of supernatural immunity.

No wonder the psalmist declared:

Psalm 91:3

Surely he shall deliver thee from the snare of the fowler, and from the noisome pestilence.

This verse gives us even more insight into the unparalleled advantages of being in the Secret Place. You see, a fowler is one who hunts birds. We know that a bird is meant for flight, but if captured in a snare, it is not strong enough to escape. Also, in scripture, the soul is often likened to a bird. In Psalm 124, verse 7, the psalmist says:

Psalm 124:7

Our soul has escaped as a bird from the snare of the fowlers; The snare is broken, and we have escaped.

So you see, this is not just about birds; it's about you – your soul. There is an enemy of the soul, one who sets his traps in secret. He carefully covers or disguises his traps in hopes that the gullible soul won't perceive it. But you are not susceptible to his traps in the Secret Place.

The Bible says "He" shall deliver you. That "He" is the Lord Jesus Christ, the Secret Place. And the word that is translated as 'deliver' is *natsal,* which means *to snatch away, preserve, defend, escape, without fail.* In the Secret Place, you are delivered – snatched away, preserved, defended, and you escaped – from every snare of the enemy *without fail.* There is no chance – zero possibility – of this not happening. So now you can understand why we say you are heavenly protected, heavenly guarded, heavenly defended, God protected. The snare is broken, which means crushed or destroyed. You are in the Secret Place super dozer, which crushes and destroys every snare.

In the Secret Place, it is not like you are in a place where you can be trapped, and then you escape. No! No trap can get in there! That's the point. How can the enemy get in there to set any traps? Where could he possibly get access to enter? Watch what it says in Job chapter 28:

Job 28:7-8

There is a path which no fowl knoweth, and which the vulture's eye hath not seen: The lion's whelps have not trodden it, nor the fierce lion passed by it.

Don't let your soul lie to you. Don't allow people or the media to lie to you. Don't permit your circumstances to lie to you. You are untouchable! You are in a place where the devil cannot even find you. He does not know your address because you are in a spiritual place. The vulture's eye cannot see it, neither can the fierce lion pass by it. You are in a spiritual place. Understand that the devil is a spiritual being, but he is not spiritual. Therefore, he cannot locate the Secret Place.

The devil is not the only one that cannot find you in the
Secret Place. I want you to notice what it says a few verses
down in verses 22 and 23:

Job 28:22-23

**Destruction and death say, We have heard the
fame   thereof   with   our   ears.   God
understandeth   the   way   thereof,   and   he
knoweth the place thereof.**

Your soul may have tried to convince you that you are a
wide-open target. You are not. You are in the Secret Place
where not even destruction and death can find you. They
even testify that they have heard about this Place, but they
can't see it, brother! They cannot enter there, sister! Death
and destruction cannot understand how to get to that
location. You are in the Secret Place, and only God can put
you in there. He understands the way because He *is* the
Way! Evil is prohibited there. You can fly freely; you can
soar to heights unimaginable! Oh, Glory be to God!

The psalmist declares that you are snatched away –
delivered – from the "noisome pestilence." Right now, the
world is in an uproar because of COVID-19. There are
booster shots upon booster shots, and every time you turn
around, they are announcing a "new variant." They want
you to be covered by their worldly solutions and devices.
But we have something superior to any solution the world
could offer. You are covered in the Secret Place.

Psalm 91:4

He shall cover you with His feathers, and under His wings you shall take refuge; His truth shall be your shield and buckler.

So many times, we hear or think of the word 'cover,' and we think only of something overhead. Yes, a covering includes that too, but your feet can be covered; your back can be covered; your hands can be covered. Do you see? The covering of the Secret Place is absolute. In fact, the word rendered "cover" literally means *to fence in*. You are in a Place of protection and defence; you are *shut up* in Christ. The Apostle Paul put it this way in Colossians chapter 3:

Colossians 3:3

For ye are dead, and your life is hid [*hidden, concealed, kept secret*, emphasis added] with Christ in God.

Dead people don't worry about bills; they don't concern themselves with what is going on in the world's economy or the market fluctuations. Dead people are not concerned about getting sick or dying. In Christ, the Secret Place, you are dead to those things. More importantly, your life now is hidden in the Secret Place. The truth you know about the Secret Place is your defence, your shield and buckler. You are covered, and no part of you is left uncovered; no part of your life is vulnerable. Your health is covered; your business, your finances, your children, *you are covered*!

No matter the variant, the strain, the virus, the mutation, you reside in a place where disease is demolished. You do not need to be afraid. Psalm 91, verses 5 through 7 tells you this:

Psalm 91:5-7

Thou shalt not be afraid for the terror by night; nor for the arrow that flieth by day; Nor for the pestilence that walketh in darkness; nor for the destruction that wasteth at noonday. A thousand shall fall at thy side, and ten thousand at thy right hand; but it shall not come nigh thee.

A lot of wickedness is carried out in the night. This "night" does not refer to physical darkness only. A person's mind can be in the night, their deeds can be in darkness, and their understanding can be darkened. There is a certain terror that comes to those who are in darkness. But that is not where you are. The Bible says that our everyday reality ought to be walking or living in the light even as He is in the light (1 John 1:7). Notice what it says in 1 John chapter 1 and verse 5:

1 John 1:5

This then is the message which we have heard of him, and declare unto you, that God is light, and in him is no darkness at all.

You are in the Secret Place where there is no kind of darkness at all, not the darkness of the mind, nor the darkness of understanding or lack of revelation. You know the truth, and it is making you free right this minute.

You won't need to be afraid of the dark anymore nor fear the dangers of the day. He did not say there are no dangers in the daytime. He says you do not fear the dangers of the day. Why? Because the Lord already told you He takes care of you. You dwell in the Secret Place of the Most High. You abide under the shadow of The Almighty. He spreads His feathers, His wings, over you, and you are under His cover.

Then He says even though a thousand shall fall at thy side, and ten thousand are dying around you, evil will not touch you. Once again, He did not say nothing would happen on your right hand or on your left. He acknowledges that there is so much evil and trouble, so many crises happening. But what is important is that "it shall not come nigh thee." You are in a place of divine protection.

The saints of old searched for this place, but it was reserved for us. The Bible says of Abraham that he sought a city whose builder and maker is God.

Hebrews 11:8, 10

By faith Abraham, when he was called to go out into a place which he should after receive for an inheritance, obeyed; and he went out, not knowing whither he went … For he looked for a city which hath foundations, whose builder and maker is God.

The city Abraham searched for is located in the Secret Place. The Bible calls it Mount Zion. Remember, in Christ there are locations. Mount Zion is one of them. This is not a place that you need to march towards. The Bible declares that you are already there. This is what it says in Hebrews chapter 12, verses 22 to 24, which reads as follows:

Hebrews 12:22-24a

But ye are come unto mount Sion, and unto the city of the living God, the heavenly Jerusalem, and to an innumerable company of angels, to the general assembly and church of the firstborn, which are written in heaven, and to God the Judge of all, and to the spirits of just men made perfect, and to Jesus the mediator of the new covenant

Did you catch that? Coming to Mount Zion is the same as coming to Jesus because Mount Zion is real estate in the Secret Place, which is Christ Himself. That is where you are. I want you to see and understand the reality of the Place you are in. What else is in there? How fortified is it? Let's go a little further into Psalm 91 and take a look.

The psalmist said that in the Secret Place, you are protected by angels. We see this in Psalm 91, verses 10 and 11:

Psalm 91:10-11

No evil shall befall you, nor shall any plague come near your dwelling; for He shall give His angels charge over you, to keep you in all your ways.

I want you to come into the awareness of just how protected you are, even in Mount Zion, which is inside the Secret Place. Live in the consciousness of it. Remember, the Bible says that you live, move, and have your being in the Secret Place. That means you are there right now, whether at work, on a bus, or wherever. You are in the Secret Place. What's more, you are not alone. Angels are surrounding you, guarding you as you go about your daily affairs, in that aeroplane, in your car, in your house, as you sleep. You are guarded by angels.

You might have thought you had to become a famous celebrity to have bodyguards here on Earth, but you have them right now. And these are no small beings. These are mighty angels! The next verse gives you a clue about just how mighty they are.

Psalm 91:12

In their hands they shall bear you up, Lest you dash your foot against a stone.

Think how mighty an angel must be to hold you up in their hands. This is not just an angel that catches you if you trip so that you won't fall. In their "hands" means in the hollow of their hands. These angels can carry you in the palm of their hands! They are your angelic guards who act as watchmen to make sure your journey in life is free of terror. Not one, not two, but an "innumerable company of angels!"

I want you to see what the psalmist declares about this glorious real estate you inhabit. Watch what it says in Psalm 48, verses 12 and 13:

Psalm 48:12-13

**Walk about Zion, and go round about her: tell
the towers thereof. Mark ye well her
bulwarks, consider her palaces; that ye may
tell it to the generation following.**

The psalmist invites you to lift up your eyes and see where
you are. Check it out. You are in the city of the living God, a
place where your greatness is manifested, and where all its
inhabitants are thoroughly protected. It says consider her
bulwarks and see that you are in a place of maximum
security. There are no vulnerabilities in its borders. Its
bulwarks cannot be breached. Its perimeter cannot be
penetrated. You are in a well-fortified place.

Furthermore, Mount Zion is inside Christ, the Secret Place.
You cannot get any more secure than that! That is why the
psalmist in verse 13 of Psalm 91 declared:

Psalm 91:13

**Thou shalt tread upon the lion and adder: the
young lion and the dragon shalt thou trample
under feet.**

This is remarkable! Why are you able to tread on the lion
and adder and dragon? It is because you are in the Secret
Place. You will see it when I take you to 1 Corinthians 15,
verse 27.

1 Corinthians 15:27

For he hath put all things under his feet.

I know you thought Psalm 91, verse 13 was talking about your feet only, but always be conscious that you are in the Secret Place. And the Bible declares that all things have been put under Christ's feet. You are walking in Christ, and Christ has already walked all over the devil and anything else that could harm you.

No wonder the psalmist declared, "Glorious things are spoken of thee, O city of God!" (Psalm 87:3). And here's the best part. He's not doing this because you've done everything right, or because you pray for hours or fast every other day. Your right to dwell in the Secret Place is based on one thing: His love for you.

Love is the invitation into the Secret Place. If you are not conscious of anything else, be conscious of His love for you. Knowing that He loves you, that perfect love casts out every fear. Love is the language, culture, and atmosphere of the Secret Place. It's all about intimacy with Christ.

When you consciously live by the revelation of the Secret Place, you operate by a different set of rules. You don't fear anything, not even death. Right now, the whole world is crying out for fear, fear of sickness, disease, and death. But in the Secret Place, you are assured of long life.

Psalm 91 ends with a glorious triumphant note of victory over the world's most dreaded enemy, death. Note what the psalmist declares in verse 16:

Psalm 91:16

With long life will I satisfy him, and shew him my salvation.

Now, I want you to see something here, and step into this reality by faith. It says God will satisfy you with "long" life. He's not talking about allowing you to live a hundred years or one hundred and twenty years. What would be so special about that when people who don't even know God live as long as that? What He's talking about is a special status reserved only for those in the Secret Place.

The word translated 'long' comes from the Hebrew word *órek*, and it means *forever*! I know your soul has been programmed all these years to believe you're supposed to grow old and die. With every birthday, people want to know how old you are. When you reach a certain milestone in years, the world automatically begins to refer to you as a "senior citizen." You work, and after some years they tell you that you should prepare to "retire," cease to work. Then you wonder why your mind ceases to work, and your bones cease to work, and your outlook and vision cease to work. Reject this mentality. There is something superior for the Secret Place dwellers – a *forever* life, a life of fullness, a satisfied life!

Brothers and sisters, the Secret Place is a mindset. That means you can decide from this very moment, I'm not dying, and I refuse to "grow old." Tell yourself, I will never be sick another day in my life! My bones will function, and none of my organs or systems will fail to operate optimally. You can tell that sickness you have no business being in my body because I live in the Secret Place. Speak to that business, that marriage, that womb, that ministry, and command it to flourish inside the Secret Place. Always be conscious that you are in the Supernatural Super Dozer called Christ. And walk in the confidence of the security, protection, provision, and preservation of the Secret Place.

TEN

THE ULTIMATE 9-1-1

This past February marked the fifty-third anniversary of 9-1-1. And when I say "9-1-1," I'm not referring to the date or tragedy that occurred on September 11th. Instead, I am referring to the three-digit telephone number that has been designated as the Universal Emergency Number for citizens throughout the United States to request emergency assistance. The UK actually came up with the concept of an emergency service number twenty years earlier, in 1937, then other countries followed suit. Now "9-1-1" has become a universal standard and phrase to refer to an emergency situation.

The UK may have been the first to enact an emergency number for its citizens, but it was not the originator. God was. He wanted His people to have a number that we could use to get emergency assistance, something that we can refer to and remember whenever we are in need. So He gave us His own version of 9-1-1 – Psalm 91:1.

The emergency number system to which we have become accustomed here on Earth functions very much like God's

9-1-1. In general, it is designed to be used for situations involving an immediate threat of serious injury to life or property. However, as we take a closer look at the emergency system that is local to Earth, we will clearly see the superiority of God's Secret Place 9-1-1 system.

No Delay

Have you ever wondered what would happen if you called 9-1-1 and no one answered? It does happen. Sometimes the 9-1-1 service experiences an outage, or you could pick up your phone only to find there is no dial tone. Another possible scenario is you might have called at the precise moment a shift change is taking place, and no one is available to take your call. After all, local 9-1-1 dispatchers are human; they get tired and need to go home and rest. In such instances, there is no way to know if the call is a life-threatening situation or not. That means there is a chance someone is experiencing harm, or even dying, due to the delay. Those are some of the limitations you face when you're dealing with the local 9-1-1 emergency service.

God's Secret Place 9-1-1, on the other hand, has no such issues. No shift change needs to take place because our God does not get tired. The Bible says He neither slumbers nor sleeps. He is always available and ready to answer the call. Furthermore, His line is open 24 hours a day, every single day of the year. And so, it is guaranteed that He will be the One you're going to talk to on the other side of the call.

We have access to His emergency services at the snap of a finger, in real time. There is no delay whatsoever. The line rings directly to Psalm 91, verse 1, the Secret Place. And you can rest assured that you will never get a busy signal or a recording that God's 9-1-1 service is "temporarily unavailable." He can answer billions of calls all at the same time, and He answers them personally. He is the Ultimate Dispatcher! That brings us to another distinction between the local 9-1-1 and the Secret Place 9-1-1.

The Nature of Your Emergency

Let's assume that you manage to get through to the local emergency service, and someone actually answers on the other end. The first thing you're going to notice is that a dispatcher answers. And when the dispatcher answers, there is no time for small talk. They immediately want to know one thing and one thing only: *What is the nature of your emergency?* They need to get to the reason for your call right away so that they'll know how to direct the emergency. For example, if it's a fire, they'll dispatch the fire brigade. If someone requires medical attention, an ambulance will be dispatched. If the caller is afraid someone is trying to break into their home, the police will be alerted.

However, when you use the Secret Place 9-1-1 system, you find that God, the Divine Dispatcher, does not need to ask the nature of your emergency. He already knows everything. But the protocol of the emergency system dictates that the emergency and its location be communicated by voice between the caller and the call taker. So, God, as the Call Taker, waits for you to speak and make your requests known.

Phillipians 4:6

... Let your requests be made known to God.

And when you speak, He wants you to be specific as you pray and declare things.

After you have specified the nature of your emergency, emergency *verses* are dispatched to you. The Divine Dispatcher expects you to use His Word to speak to your specific situation, understanding that in the Secret Place, as you speak, things happen.

Are anxiety and stress trying to get a hold of you? Don't worry. Verse 2 has been dispatched immediately. Have you suddenly lost your vision? Verses 5, 11, and 12 are right there. Are you experiencing confusion? Remain calm. Verse 4 is at your door. Are you alarmed because you have tested positive for COVID-19 or been diagnosed with cancer or some other "terminal" illness? Verses 5 through 7, 10 and 16 have already been dispatched. Does your business appear to be floundering, or does your financial situation look grim? Verses 7, 8, 14, and 15 are exactly what you need. Whatever the perceived threat, injury, or loss you have sustained, your solution is in the Secret Place. You need only speak to that mountain.

Dedicated Professionals

The first thing you need to understand is that when you call your local 9-1-1, you set a lot of people in motion. There are anywhere from one to one hundred people ready to serve you at any given time. So in your city, you know there are up to at least one hundred people standing by just in case you have an emergency. Those are reassuring stats, but nothing to compare with God's ultimate 9-1-1.

Now, when it comes to our Divine Dispatcher, the moment you speak things into the atmosphere, a flurry of activity is set in motion. In His emergency system, you do not have regular emergency personnel like firefighters and paramedics. Instead, you have angels, and we're not talking about one or even one hundred angels. According to Hebrews 12, verse 22, you have "an innumerable company of angels." In other words, there are so many, you can't even count them. Imagine that!

The local 9-1-1 is limited in resources. That means if multiple emergencies are occurring at the same time, the dispatcher may even come up shorthanded. But when we come to the Divine Dispatcher, He places unlimited resources at your disposal. You have emergency services in the form of angelic beings. These angels are stronger than any policemen who could arrive on the scene, more fearless than any firemen sent to help you, and more skilled than any paramedic.

You see, The God of the Ultimate 9-1-1 has the highest number of dedicated personnel, and there are never any staff shortages. He dispatches angelic paramedics that can perform miracles right there on the spot. They don't need fancy machines, and they don't need an ambulance. They arrive at the speed of thought. They don't get tired; they don't complain; they don't need sick days and are not intimidated by anything. They are ready, willing, and able to be of assistance to you. So, not only are verses dispatched to you, but certain angels are also dispatched, ready to carry out or make happen the things you declare. These are dedicated professionals who will see to it that you get the help you need.

You see, angels respond to the Word Himself, the Divine Dispatcher, and when you speak, they recognize that the Word is speaking through you. When you understand the Secret Place revelation, you know that anything you say will happen. You have the mandate because you have Christ in you, the hope of glory. He's alive on the inside of you. Everything you see, it is Him who is seeing it. When you talk, He is talking on the inside of you. Everything becomes certain, and everything becomes sure, because He is communicating from inside you.

Stay on the Line

Now, a specific protocol must be followed both in the local 9-1-1 and in the Secret Place 9-1-1. When you call 9-1-1, one of the rules is you must stay on the line. In other words, you must remain connected to the source. The dispatcher will advise you to stay calm and assure you that help is on the way.

In the Secret Place 9-1-1, angels are immediately dispatched after you make your request known and speak to the situation. However, you are still required to stay on the line. Understand that God is the ultimate Dispatcher, and while you are on the line with Him, He has heard you speak to that mountain. If the mountain is sickness, you have told the mountain to move. If the mountain is your failing business, you have already spoken, and the mountain has moved. But you must stay on the line with the Dispatcher. Or in other words, stay in the Word. Why? Because He wants you to be aware, and have that consciousness, that as long as you are in the Secret Place, which is Christ, there is no way the devil can touch you no matter what he tries to do. And this is the thing with our Dispatcher: He has the ability to answer the call, direct your emergency, and also be where you are, all at the same time.

100% Success Rate

Inevitably, there are times when the local 9-1-1 will answer the call, dispatch the emergency responders, do everything right, but they still fail. There is a chance that when the medical personnel get to you, even if they get there on time, they still can't get you out of the crisis you are in. Or they might get to you, but due to human error, they make a mistake, and instead of helping, they make the situation worse. But when you call the Ultimate Dispatcher, He never misses. He's made provision to get you out of that trouble, and His success rate is one hundred per cent.

Even before you call Him, He has given you something to confront the situation. You have a double-edged sword that is alive in you. All you have to do is speak with the understanding that the sword is the Word of God – the Word in you, Christ in you, the Secret Place in you.

Know Your Location

Stay with me as we conclude on this subject with these analogies.

Yet another protocol that must be followed with 9-1-1 emergency services: you must know your location. Identifying your location is absolutely essential to the success of the 9-1-1 service. With 9-1-1 emergency service, nothing is going to work unless they know your location. They cannot dispatch anyone to you if they cannot locate you. So, they depend on their GPS as well as you knowing what city you are in, or the address, cross streets, and any other information you can offer about your location. They need you to help their dispatched emergency personnel find you.

However, there are instances where your situation may be so dire that you are unable to know, remember, or articulate your location. Even if they could track you via your mobile signal, your battery could die before they get your location. And even with the most sophisticated satellite mapping and GPS locators, the local 9-1-1 tracking system can fail. It can be affected by something as simple as a downed power line or radio interference. Or it may just not be precise enough to identify your exact location.

Being able to identify and communicate where you are is also critical to God's 9-1-1 emergency service. He knows where you are because He is everywhere, and He knows everything. But this protocol is dependent on you – your understanding of the revelation of the Secret Place. Therefore, you must always be conscious of your location in Christ.

Whenever you have an emergency, remember your location. When people slander you or look down on you, the moment the doctor gives you a bad report, or your boss tells you you're fired, or whenever there is an apparent threat of harm or injury to your life, property, or anything that concerns you, remember your location. Tell the bearer of bad news, thank you, sir, for the information. Thank you, ma'am, for giving your input. But right now, I'm going to make a 9-1-1 call. And then remind yourself of God's 9-1-1: *"He who dwells in the Secret Place of the Most High." That's me! I dwell in the Secret Place. I walk in it. I function in it. I function in Him who is on the inside of me!*

Know your location. Christ is alive in you. Everywhere you go, He's with you. Everything you do, He's with you. No matter what comes your way, He's with you. You are in the Secret Place. You don't get perturbed, depressed, or stressed out. That happens to people who don't understand the magnitude of the Person they carry. When you understand how big He is, you know that nothing shall touch you.

You are in a mighty fortress, a well-fortified place. You are not intimidated by any circumstance because God's emergency service – His 9-1-1 Secret Place – is in you. And everything that you're going through, not only does He hear it, He also does something about it. So be conscious of this reality, and practice having the Secret Place in you.

But if in a moment of crisis, your heart is overwhelmed, and you have a temporary lapse of consciousness, God's GPS can still locate you wherever you are. His tracking system is accurate to a tee. No matter where you are, He can locate you. He can zoom in on you with 100 per cent accuracy and pick you up from wherever you are.

You can never go so far that you are out of His reach. In fact, He made you with a biological and spiritual GPS system. So wherever you are, He can see right through your spirit, soul, and body. That means He can locate you spiritually, "soulically," and physically. He knows whether you are a babe in Christ or you are mature spiritually. That's the kind of GPS He uses – the ultimate GPS. He knows the exact situation you're going through before you even pray. And even while you are still speaking, He's already answered, and there is no way He can lose your signal. Your local 9-1-1 may not have all the answers, but the Ultimate Dispatcher has all the solutions you need, and He can get them to you at any given moment.

No Prank Calls

Now, there is one last and fundamental 9-1-1 rule that I must share with you. When you call the 9-1-1 emergency services, never hang up. Even if you dialled by mistake, don't hang up. Local emergency dispatchers do not take kindly to accidental 9-1-1 calls. For that reason, they advise you not to program 9-1-1 into your phone's speed dial. And if you made the mistake of dialling 9-1-1, they want you to delete it from your recent history so that you minimize the chance of accidentally redialling it. They do not want you to test to see if 9-1-1 is working. And in all their literature, they caution you that 9-1-1 is not a toy.

If you mistakenly dial your local 9-1-1, they would rather you stay on the line and tell them it was a mistake rather than just hanging up. Why? Because if there is an actual emergency, they would rather err on the side of caution. So, if you hang up, they will assume there's a real emergency and come to your location anyway.

Prank calling, or even accidentally dialling 9-1-1, is no joke. Not only does prank or accidental 9-1-1 calling waste time and money, calling 9-1-1 for a non-emergency could also result in a hefty fine and imprisonment. In the UK, you could face a maximum *penalty* of up to six months in prison or a *fine* of £5,000 for a prank call to emergency services. But even more importantly than jail time or a fine, if 9-1-1 dispatchers are having to deal with a prank or accidental call, someone who has a real emergency might not be able to get the help they need.

Always remember that a call to 9-1-1 is for emergency purposes only. And so, God is looking at your growth as a Christian, and He is expecting you to understand the Secret Place revelation and use it to your benefit. That means, before you rush to call God's 9-1-1, know that you have a sword.

Now the sword you were given is a weapon that is unlike anything that has ever been seen. It is not a weapon of mass destruction; it is a weapon of mass deliverance. What's more, that weapon is inside you in the form of God's Word. Now that you understand the revelation of the Secret Place, instead of rushing to call for help from the Dispatcher, speak the Word with the consciousness that as you speak, Christ is speaking. That is how you use the sword of the Word of God.

The writer of Hebrews calls it a "double-edged" sword. The fact that the Word is a double-edged sword means it can cut in any direction. Whatever the problem – whether it be financial, sickness, relationship, mental, or other – the sword is going to work. Use it without fail, understanding the revelation that Christ is in you and that He is the Secret Place, and you dwell in Him.

Be conscious of where you are. You dwell in the Secret Place. That means you are in Christ right now; you are in heavenly places in Him. You live, move, and have your being in the Secret Place. That means the radius of your home is a no-fly zone for witches and demonic entities. No trouble can come near you. The moment you step into any environment, you carry the Secret Place with you and take over! No prank calls are necessary.

Easy to Remember

The final thing that makes the local emergency number system work so well is that 9-1-1 is so easy to remember. You have only three simple digits that even a young child can commit to memory. So even during a panic or stress-inducing situation, you are cognizant of the fact that there is a simple way to get help when you need it.

That is also the power of God's ultimate 9-1-1. You need only be mindful of one thing: the Secret Place is in me, and I am in Him. How wonderful is this God for giving you such a simple method for accessing whatever you need whenever you need it! He was not satisfied just visiting you or having you meet Him in certain locations at certain times. He wants to be in the thick of things, involved in every detail of your life. So He decided to be in every single person who accepts Him as their Secret Place.

Now, you carry God. He is with you at all times – when you go to court, when you sit an exam, during that drive, when you are in the doctor's office, as you do your business. He is right there in every single matter and every detail of your life. The Secret Place is God's ultimate response to you.

This is a dimension-shifting revelation. Think about it. Be conscious of it. This is not a reality that you visit every now and then. No. Now, you are intermingled with Him. This is your lifestyle. Practice it. Tell yourself, the Secret Place is in me right now, and I am in Him. Keep saying it until everything you are – your consciousness, your mindset, your body – is completely immersed in that revelation.

When you live in the consciousness of the revelation of the Secret Place, it changes everything! How can you possibly fail when you live in the Secret Place and the Secret Place is in you? Tell yourself, *I can never be broke another day in my life, impossible! I am a success! Nothing I do will ever fail. I carry the Secret Place, God's Ultimate 9-1-1. Wherever I go, things will work there. If I start a business, it will work. If I'm involved in a business, it will work better. He is with me when I sleep and when I awake. He is with me when I walk; He is with me when I talk. Wherever I am, I can declare a thing at any time, and it happens right away.* Why? Because Christ, the Secret Place, is in you!

Let this revelation not be like other words that you've heard and done nothing about. Practice it until the Secret Place is personified in you. This is the highest privilege we have ever received in our lives; the highest honour is to carry the Secret Place. You no longer need to wait for His manifest presence. You no longer have to find a mountain or ravine to find that Secret Place. You are saturated, fully immersed, in His Presence. Let it become a reality in you; be conscious of it. And let this mindset take root in you that, finally, you understand that the Secret Place is in you, and you are in Him.

ABOUT THE AUTHOR

Madam Beverly "BeBe" Angel is one of the most visible prophetic leaders of our time. Together with her husband, His Excellency Ambassador Uebert Angel, they are the founders of the ever-growing Spirit Embassy The Good News Church worldwide. She is a bestselling author, international speaker, and well-seasoned entrepreneur. She is also the visionary and founder of Core100, A Christian sisterhood, mentorship, and accountability community.

A devoted wife and mother of four boys, Madam Bebe also serves with her husband as patron of their charity arm, the Uebert Angel Foundation, whose primary aim is to demonstrate the love of Christ through practical giving to those in need.

Connect with Madam BeBe Angel at beverlyangel.org

ALSO BY BEVERLY UEBERT ANGEL

Enjoy Life Now: Biblical Secrets to Enjoying Life on a Daily Basis

Intimacy: How to Become a Best Friend and Lover of God

Grace Driven Life: Proven Steps to Living a Guilt-Free Life

Available at:

beverlyangel.org

Amazon.com

Wherever Books Are Sold